W9-BLO-547

PRESENTATIONS For PROFITS

Dozens of ways to increase bookings at Home Party demonstrations

Christie Northrup
The Lemon Aid Lady

Cover design by Steve James

Lemon Aid Learning Adventures
Dallas, Texas 75065
www.lemonaidlady.com

Published by Lemon Aid Learning Adventures™

Presentations for Profit$. Copyright 2003 by Christie Northrup. All rights reserved. No portion of this book may be reproduced, stored in a retrieval system, or transmitted in any form or by any means—electronic, mechanical, photocopy, recording, or any other—except for brief quotations in printed reviews, without the prior written permission of the author.

Printed in the United States of America

ISBN: 1-930182-03-1

DEDICATION

You would not be reading this book—which took nearly twenty-five years to write—if my life had not been touched by hundreds of dedicated people. Sometimes, leaders are the last to be recognized and appreciated. Therefore, this book is first dedicated to three couples who were my sales leaders, mentors, and inspiration. Each taught me something different, yet synergistic. Many of the ideas you'll read in this book came from the seeds they planted in my heart and mind.

- Valerie and Duane Bills, Skyline Sales, Salt Lake City, Utah
- Pattie and John Chwalek, Venture Sales, Garden City, Michigan
- Bonnie and Ken Tumey, Star-Brite Sales, Saginaw, Michigan

TABLE OF CONTENTS
Scripts are listed in bold face

INTRODUCTION

When the general population hears the words, "home party," what's the first thing that comes to mind? Feeling the pressure to buy, having to clean house for an event, and even blunt words such as "don't even ask me" are a few of the thoughts and feelings commonly expressed. But for those who become frequent hostesses, the terms "fun," "gifts," "shopping," and "friends" are heard. Home parties sometimes have an initial bad reputation--not because of the party plan concept or the company, in most cases, but more often because of the demonstrators. Likewise, thousands of people have been sold on the concept of the home party marketing plan because of dynamic, customer-focused demonstrators.

I vividly remember my first home party experience as an adult--I was in college and anxious to attend. The presenter looked as if she had just walked in from a Physical Education class. She was dressed in tight, black sweat pants and a baggy T-shirt. The only thing I remember, besides her appearance, was her saying she had to "...take the spaghetti out of the bowls to bring them to the party." Well, I could see and smell where the spaghetti had been in the bowl. My first thought was "I better not order those bowls, they might come with her spaghetti--or at least with the stains and smell--already in them!"

The next year I was a married woman. My co-worker, Margo, begged me to "...please book a party so I can get my free picnic cooler." (I soon discovered "begging" is one ploy many consultants use for booking more parties.) I really didn't care if Margo got her cooler, but I liked Margo, so I reluctantly agreed. I don't remember hearing from the demonstrator until the day of the party. I think she did give me some invitations and catalogs beforehand, but I didn't know what to do with them so I tossed them. I really did not want to have a party, but I felt obligated (the byproduct of begging) to help my friend.

I love to cook and entertain. But for this party, I remember stopping at the corner grocery and picking up some Keebler® cookies. I hadn't invited anyone. Rather, I begged (people who book from begging usually beg—not invite—people to come) my next-door neighbor just to show up so I wouldn't be embarrassed. When the cute demonstrator got to my apartment (she really was a very nice lady), she commented that I could also get the same kind of cooler as Margo if I got a dollar amount in sales and some other people to host party parties! I was certainly flabbergasted!! I thought getting the big cooler was like winning the lottery – only a chosen person or two would win. I had no idea I could get the same kind of gifts as Margo. So, I got on the phone, got the sales and the bookings to win my own cooler. It was then I began to understand the "home party" concept – I thought it was pretty cool.

Another year passed. By then I was a new mom with a darling infant son. My husband had his first job out of college, and we decided it was time to buy a home. But we had a slight problem: we didn't have enough money. This was in the early 1980s, when interest rates were rapidly rising daily. We thought if we didn't buy a house at that moment, we'd never be homeowners. I had quit my full-time job to be a full-time mom. After about three months of being on a "honeymoon with my baby," I was a little bored and a lot broke. I was in pursuit of something I could do to make money and stay home—a novel concept for that era. But what was I going to do? Staying at home with a baby *and make money*? This idea was too good to be true.

Because I love to cook, I thought of opening a catering business or doing cake decorating. So, with the encouragement of my supportive husband, I enrolled in a class on cake decorating. It's a good thing I didn't invest a lot of time or money on that venture as I'm creative, but not artistic. I decided to keep the cake decorating for the family occasions. But aside from babysitting for other moms, I couldn't think of any other way to make money and be at home.

About that same time, I got a call from my favorite former boss at the University Press, Norm Darais. He informed me that my replacement was leaving to study abroad, and invited me to come back to work, which I did. Looking back, I am so sad I hadn't met someone from a party plan company at that time. Something inside of me was saying I could combine work with motherhood. Initially, I took the baby to work everyday. But as he grew, I soon realized that an office is not a place for a baby, and reluctantly had to hire a sitter. My husband and I cried every morning when we left our son in the care of someone else. Fortunately, I only did this for a few months.

The next year we moved across the country. I attended another home party from that same company that impressed me with the picnic cooler; back then, not many party plan companies were in

I was a little bored and a lot broke. I was in pursuit of something I could do to make money and stay home—a novel concept for that era. Staying at home with a baby and make money? This idea was too good to be true.

existence. Because of the move, our funds were again limited, but I bought several products at the party and had a lot of fun. During the party, I wrote down some new items on the order form so I wouldn't forget the prices—I did it for my reference, not to order. When the consultant collected the order forms, she added those new items to my order. When I attempted to explain to her what I had done, she snapped back at me, saying I had done the order incorrectly and was wasting her time. Obviously, I wasn't impressed. Even though she was *nicely dressed*, she wasn't *nice*.

She then asked me to be a hostess (actually, she *attacked* me to be a hostess). I explained I was living at my in-law's home until we moved into our apartment (my mother-in-law would have loved me to have invited company over, but I had to think of some excuse!). All the while, I sent signals indicating I needed money. And I was a new mom who needed to get out of the house. But she never invited to be a consultant.

I did not know that people earned money doing home parties. I mistakenly thought the company would give me product for selling their stuff.

Six months passed. My husband was doing well in his new job; we had our own apartment. Life was great – except I was climbing the walls. I needed something to do to get out of the house. One day, my young son and I were baking cookies--it was St. Patrick's Day, 1980. As I was using the Tupperware® mixing bowls, measuring cups, and canisters I had received as wedding gifts, I thought, "I really need more of this stuff. Maybe, I could be one of those ladies and get some of this free." You see, I did not know that people earned *money* doing home parties. I mistakenly thought the company would give me *product* for selling their stuff. So, I picked up the phone, dialed a long-distance number and asked for information on the company and its selling opportunities. The woman on the other end of the phone assured me that "someone would contact me." I assumed I'd get something in the mail within four to six weeks. I was patient. I was willing to wait. That same day the phone rang. It was Jeanne.

Jeanne was a vivacious, excited, professional woman. She told me how lucky I was that I had called that day because the following day was a big meeting. She had me so excited to attend--even though it was in another city. I had no car, no baby sitter--but I said YES. Jeanne had gotten me so excited about the meeting, I thought the president of the company was going to be at this big event; I didn't want to miss it. When I asked her what I should wear, she replied: "Wear what you'd wear to church." I was so excited that I had an excuse to dress up in my "former life" clothes – a business suit.

At my first direct sales meeting the next morning, I was totally impressed and excited! When I walked in the room, I met Bonnie and Ken Tumey – the sales leaders. Bonnie looked at me, and with a big smile said, "You look so sharp!" And I thought: "Wow! A compliment. I like this! When can I come back?" At this meeting, I saw bonus checks handed out, gifts given, and recognition paid. I could visualize me doing this. And, my most amazing discovery, people actually were paid in cash – not products!

I share this story with you to illustrate how important it is to position sales meetings to new people. Jeanne described it as a big event, which it was, even though it was just a regular weekly meeting. Through the years, after attending these meetings on a regular basis, I took them for granted. Now, I realize I should have always seen these occasions through the eyes of a new person, to maintain the excitement. Also, the compliment Bonnie paid me has stayed with me all these years – the power of positive words!

When I started in this industry, my biggest obstacle was learning how to schedule demonstrations. And through the years of teaching thousands of home-party consultants, I know this is a major challenge for everyone else.

I officially began my business on April 1, 1980. Over the next 16 years with the same company, I literally learned from the best. I met thousands of other top-notch, friendly, fun, and inspiring people. I had the privilege of working with two other sales leaders in other areas of the country: Pattie Chwalek in Detroit, Michigan. She taught me the importance of close communication with my team coupled with superb customer service. And in Salt Lake City, Utah I worked with Valerie Bills. Valerie taught me how to be bold in thinking, dreaming, and teaching. My team did amazing things under her leadership. As a result of the collective tutelage of these great sales leaders, my personal team rose to national prominence. That's why I've dedicated this book to these three women. However, thousands of other consultants and sales leaders also had a great influence on me.

When I started in this industry, my biggest obstacle was learning how to schedule demonstrations. And through the years of teaching thousands of home-party consultants, I know this is a major challenge for everyone else. My biggest "ah-ha!" came as I was driving to a sales meeting where I was to give a talk on bookings. At that moment, an inspiration came to me that when I give a demonstration, people are really learning from me – I'm a teacher, not a salesperson. When I realized this, I thought, "I have such great ideas to share with people to help them; I'm a valuable resource!" That revelation was the beginning of my booking break through.

After being a consultant, manager, and distributor (the highest rank in the company) for over 16 years, I began a new company, Lemon Aid Learning Adventures™. I now have privilege of teaching consultants and representatives in all direct sales/party plan companies. In many cases, I've actually joined a company solely to research and more fully understand its culture, concept, and language. So it's no surprise that after conducting one of my live Learning Adventures for a company, many of the representatives ask "How long have you been selling with us?" I believe that, if I am to teach you, I need to speak your language. I'll explain how you can do this at your home classes later in the book.

Much of my education was gained from attending home parties as a guest and hosting them as a hostess. These experiences, coupled with years of holding five to eight parties a week and leading top teams, has given me a real *TWIST* on the home party concept. I believe it is the best way to market a product to benefit the most people. However, the biggest responsibility for a party's success lies with you, the demonstrator. Thus, my mission for writing this book is to teach you dozens and dozens of ways of attracting—not attacking—thousands of hostesses, guests and consultants through the party plan method in creative, fun, and easy-to-implement ways.

HOW TO USE THIS BOOK

As a home-party professional, you are a busy woman or man. You probably don't have time to read a book from cover to cover. That's why I write my books in reference-style format. You don't have to start at the beginning to have a happy ending! In fact, I recommend that, before you start to read the book, thumb through its pages to see which topics focus on your *Sour Situations*. Is it hard for you to start your demonstrations on time? If so, refer to the segment *Time is More Money...and More Bookings.* Do people ignore you during your presentation? Go immediately to *Featured Attractions* and *Part of the Action* segments. Got a problem remembering people's names? Read *Name Games*.

Above all, don't try to use all these ideas at one time! These are the results of more than twenty-two years of experience with hostesses, guests, and consultants. Trying to "do it all at one once" will simply frustrate both you and your audience. Rather, focus on one or two tips at a time and do the *TWIST* so the tips fit your style. Then build from there. The most valuable lessons you'll learn will not be from the words you read on the pages but from the ideas that fill your mind as you read the words and then do your own mental *TWISTS*.

Terms: In this book, *consultant, demonstrator, representative* and *presenter* all refer to the person who is booking and selling for a company. *Hostess* refers to the person who invited the demonstrator to come to her home/office/facility and is inviting her friends and acquaintances (guests, customers) to participate. While the term *home party plan* is the method of selling a product, many companies use the words *show, class, workshop* or even others. These will be used interchangeably in this book; all refer to a selling event where a product is demonstrated.

Scripts: You find valuable words to use—scripts—highlighted in a different type font and smaller margins. These are listed in the Table of Contents in bold-face for easy reference.

Gender: Because the majority of the people involved in the Party Plan industry are women, I've written the book using the female gender. If you are a male consultant reading this book, please understand that I've done this for simplicity and space, not because I'm biased in any way. My good husband, Bob, is very involved in all aspects of the direct sales industry and substituted as a consultant for me several times. Welcome to the industry and to Presentations for Profit$.

Customizing: This book was written for all involved in the Party Plan Industry. Every company is unique in their presentation, business plan, and terms. All attempts were made to keep the ideas for generic so all companies can benefit. Remember to use the Lemon Aid *TWIST* to adapt them to your company and personality. If you desire customization for your company and situation, you can contact me directly for private consulting sessions and speaking engagements. My personal phone number is 940-498-0995.

Segment One

Pre-Presentation

Who is the most excited person once a party is booked? I'm hoping the excitement level will be high for both you and your new hostess! When the hostess begins to invite her friends, believe it or not, she doesn't always receive enthusiastic "yeses" from everyone. In fact, some people may even question her decision to book a show with you because *they* don't like parties. And when *they* question her decision, *she* questions her decision. Sometimes, in rare occasions, she may actually talk herself out of being a hostess! Of course, she doesn't want to call and disappoint you right now. No, she'll wait until the *day* of the demonstration so you don't have time to be disappointed!

Cementing the Date with Communication

So, how do you keep her enthusiasm and excitement high? By *communicating* with her. Sounds simple, doesn't it? Yet, it's usually the reason most people cancel – after the booking they hear little or nothing from the consultant until the show. So, long before the party begins, let the communication flow. Start this flow with a *Thank You note* as soon as a new hostess schedules with you. My friend, Jenny Bywater, owner of The Booster (www.thebooster.com) has wonderful, inexpensive thank you cards. (If you want to call her directly, her phone number is 1-800-5JENNYB.) I routinely used her magnets that read "It's your Party" or "It's your Show." I enclosed a magnet with the *Thank You Note*, so that every time my hostess opened her fridge or went to her filing cabinet, she saw my name, company, and phone number. My goal was to have one or more of my magnets on every fridge in the county! This way, thousands of people would be advertising my business 24/7 with my magnet in their homes and offices.

If your hostess' enthusiasm wanes when she hears a negative response, and then receives a *handwritten* thank you card within a couple of days, your communicating "thank you" encourages her to keep calling more people. Many times I saw my *Thank You Note* proudly displayed in my hostess' home. I know this extra touch cemented not only the date on my calendar, but also my relationship with my hostess. Send the *Thank You Note* before the ink is dry on your calendar! And send it to her ASASB (as soon as she books) so she receives it during the time you've asked her to compose the list.

This extra touch cemented not only the date on my calendar, but also my relationship with my hostess. Send the thank you before the ink is dry on your calendar, and send it ASASB (as soon as she books)

You might say, "I send a *Thank You Note* after the party." Do that as well. But my experience taught me that when you thank someone in advance, the event is better than it would have been. My parents taught me as a young child to start my day off with a prayer. I was taught to thank God for the new day and the blessings it would bring. I discovered that when I thanked God first thing in the morning, my day went much smoother – I was thanking him for my blessings in advance, and I felt like I was more blessed because I was grateful. I once heard the statement, "The more you give thanks, the more you'll have to be thankful for."

A Great Inviting Idea

When you are scheduling the date with your new hostess, ask her if she has voice mail or an answering machine on her home phone and/or cell phone. Most people do. If she does, suggest she go right home and change the message:

> "Hello! This is _____. Leave your message so I can call you back.
>
> Have you heard the GREAT NEWS? I'm hosting a _____ (class/party/workshop/demonstration) with _____ (company name) on _____ (day and date) at _____ (time). When you leave your message, let me know who you'll be bringing with you!"

I came up with this idea when I realized nearly every hostess, at the end of the party, would say, "I can't believe I forgot to invite Emma! I see her every day and kept forgetting to invite her." Usually, as the hostess indicated, the persons forgotten were usually those closest to her! With this great inviting idea, every time someone called my hostess, they were reminded about the big event.

Who else might be calling the hostess during the time she dates a party and the time she holds it? A lot of people. A lot of people you don't know. A lot of people who don't know you.

Let's say there is a three-week period from when she books and when the party is held. During that three weeks, assume your hostess has an average of ten people who leave a message on her voice mail each week. That's 30 people. Now, how many hostesses do you have on your calendar? If the answer is ten, and they all do this simple task (which will normally increase her attendance by

2

two or three), that's 300 people who are hearing about you and your company in a three-week period. And guess what? This exposure costs you nothing!! Your hostess is thrilled because some of the people who call her might already have been invited by her. Now, each time they call they are getting another reminder. Of course, the hostess will also get calls from people who don't know her – someone calling to remind her of a fundraiser, the doctor's office reminding her of an appointment, her travel agent calling to verify her next business trip, etc. And….you're right! They're all going to hear about her party – which is your business. Think of all the people you'll be able to service who don't even know you!

Your Top 40 List

What is the number one fear of a potential hostess? When I ask that question at Lemon Aid Learning Adventures across the country, I always get the same answer: That no one will come! It's a common fear because it affects our ego. If we plan for a big event and no one (or only a few) come, our feelings are hurt. We think people don't like us. Even though grown up people are grown up, we like to feel important. So this fear, by far, is the reason many people just say "no" to being a hostess. And, this is the biggest stumbling block for many hostesses. They wonder, "Who should I invite?"

So, how do we do the *TWIST*? First, *eliminate the excuse before you encounter it.* When someone uses this excuse as an explanation, simply reply, "I have a list of 40 people who want to attend your presentation." When I used to say this to potential hostesses, they looked at me in amazement, almost saying, "How do you know my friends?" Before they could verbalize their feelings, I showed them my *Top 40 List*.

I know what you are thinking… "I have a list like that." And you probably do. It's probably just like the ones I see in most Presentation Planning Kits. It lists categories of people. Here's an example of what I've seen over the years:
Invite a:

- Teacher
- Video store clerk
- Nurse
- Fireman
- Clerk at store
- Teller at the bank
- Parents of children's friends
- PTA Member

The biggest fear of a potential hostess is that no one will come. Eliminate that excuse before you encounter it.

- Co Worker
- Spouse's co-worker

Does this look familiar? These are okay if you want to do an okay business. But if you want to have a business full of Sweet Successes and Juicy Profits, you need to do the *TWIST*!

First, remember the Number One Lemon Aid Law for Locating Leads--found in the book and tape *Where to Find Customers when you run out of Family and Friends*. (By the way, the audio album contains more updated and more detailed information than the book. The book lists more ideas than the audio album. In other words, the audio is NOT a book on tape, but rather a valuable supplement to the book and vice versa.) This law states "Know your *Products* so you'll know who your *Prospects* are." So, what does this have to do with a *Top 40 List*? Everything. (Note: creating this custom list takes some time, but it's a great exercise to keep thinking: "Who wants/needs my product, and therefore, would be excited to attend a demonstration?")

Examine…not merely look at EVERY product in your catalog. With each examination ask yourself, "Who needs/wants this product?" Let me illustrate. I have a Longaberger catalog in front of me. One of their popular baskets is for holding tissues. Everyone who has allergies needs this basket. After all, they sniffle all the time and sneeze once an hour or more! So, on my *Top 40 List*, I ask my host to invite all persons who suffer with allergies.

Now I'm looking at a catalog from The Angel Company. Their product is rubber stamps. I see several sets of butterfly stamps. On my *Top 40*, I ask my host to invite everyone who collects butterflies. Now, this could go more ways than one (which is precisely my point!). Scientists collect butterflies, kids collect butterflies, even my good friend Dotty Winkelman collects items with butterflies on them. As my hostess reads this, she thinks of several people who would really WANT the product. They now are more interested to come to a presentation because I have something they'll WANT and NEED.

One more company example. My good friend Donita with Lady Remington Jewelry® recently sent me a new catalog. If I were a hostess, I might be thinking only of friends who wear jewelry, which could limit the people I invite. However, now I have a *Top 40 List* and it includes:

- Everyone who has a dog.

- All people who love hats.
- Friends who wear fashion scarves.
- Persons with the name "Trish."
- All *Wizard of Oz* fans.

Now, let's examine why these are on my *Top 40 List*. One of the pins is a cute puppy. One is a fashion hat and another pin is a profile of a woman wearing a large brimmed hat. Several items are scarf clips or scarf tubes. One of the necklaces features the name "Trish." And for all *Wizard of Oz* fans, we would want to buy the pin that looks like Dorothy's red ruby slippers.

Update your **Top 40 List** *each time new products and catalogs are released.*

Are you doing the *TWIST*? Are you seeing how putting needs/wants of **specific** people rather than simply general groups will encourage and excite your host? I hope you noticed one more very important way I worded these specific people...I used the **plural**. Notice the words *everyone, all people, friends, person, all*.... This has them thinking of multiple people subconsciously.

Lastly, here are a few specifics that I put on every *Top 40*:

The person you scheduled your presentation from. This is the only time I use a singular term. This is also always the first person I list. Most new hostesses think the previous host she scheduled from has received all the products she wants. We know this is rarely, if ever, the case. Additionally, I do some really fun things when the previous hostess attends (see the segment on *Thank You, Two*).

Persons with a birthday the month of your presentation. You can recognize these folks.

All persons you know who are experiencing a challenging time. These are the people who really need to get out of the house! And maybe into a new business!

People who play the lottery or enter Sweepstakes. These people like to get something they don't have to pay for. They make great hosts!

And always, *persons looking for a career change* (I don't have to explain why you'll want these people to attend, do I?)

Update your *Top 40 List* each time new products and catalogs are released.

If your group or company has hired me to teach Presentations for Profit$, you might already have a *Top 40 List* that I created for you. I hope you're using it. If you don't have one, this is a service I provide when I do company-specific classes or in my Lemon Aid One-on-One consultations.

Benefits to Hostesses for Preparing a Guest List

When we write things down, we remember them. When a hostess prepares a guest list of all the people she's inviting, she can physically check the names off. When we have a wedding, shower, graduation, or other party, we create an invitation list. A home demonstration party is no different. Other benefits: You send the invitations/reminders to the guests as a service to your hostess; you get to *meet* some of the guests beforehand; you have a record for her next show; and you can use the list to build your business in ways you haven't thought of before. I'll give ideas for these benefits later.

May I ask a favor of you, my Lemon Aid Learners? For every presentation you have on your calendar as of today, please take two 20-dollar bills, go to the bank and convert them into 40 one-dollar bills. Now, if you have worked with your hostess and she has developed a strong guest list – including each guest's name, address, and phone number – and given you a copy of this list, you get to invest that money in any way you choose: savings, purchase stocks, etc.

If you have not worked with a hostess this way, and she is simply going to invite the people without this tool, take the 40 one-dollar bills, stand outside on your front porch and toss them to the wind.

I already know none of you would be so foolish as to throw money out your door like that! However, if you are not using a *Guest List* to assist your hostess and build your business, you are throwing a lot of money out the door (due to lost sales, bookings, and new recruits) and your hostesses are not having as successful presentations as they could have.

The benefits to a hostess when she uses this list are as many – if not more – than the benefits to your business. It's all in the way you present the concept to her. In addition to the Top 40 list you have created to give her ideas on who to invite, give each host a list for her to fill out. This list has room for her to put each guest's name, address, and PHONE NUMBER (please, don't forget that one). Again, the reason for collecting this information will be given as we go along.

Why have an official guest list? It keeps your hostess organized. She has plenty of space to write the information, and when she writes down the names, she is more committed to following through and calling her friends. I've discovered that many last-minute cancellations of the "no one is coming" reason is because *no one was invited*. This list also gives her a guide as she makes her calls. Teach her to code with letters:

M: Maybe she'll attend (usually a polite way of saying "no")
N: No, she won't be coming; no interest in products or ordering
O: Order because she can't make it
P: Positively will be there!
Q: Quadruple the attendance by bringing friends

Give each hostess at least two guest lists. If she has more people than will fit on one, she might not keep inviting if a list is not provided. Also, in addition to the *Top 40 List* that you have created, encourage her to have at least five to ten different zip codes (depending on the size of the area where she lives). You know that over-inviting is important, because only about 1/3 of those invited attend; another 1/3 *might* order. The last do nothing….

If your company does not provide an official list like I've discussed, you can copy one that I've created. It's very generic, and unlike some company tools that I've seen and used, it is not in duplicate form – one for the host, one for you, one for mailing labels. You'll find it in the Appendix at the back of this book.

Now that your host has an official guest list and your own *Top 40*, she can begin the writing and inviting process. For years I nearly demanded that the list be returned to me within 24 hours. Then I realized that she might have already scheduled her next 24 hours with other activities and appointments! So, I suggest you ask her, "Will you be able to write your list and invite your guests within the next three days?" Let her lead you as to when this can be completed. This just gives her some breathing room. And you don't become frustrated because the list doesn't get to you in the next couple of days.

Even though she has the *Top 40 List*, sometimes brains still cramp! I remember when my son was getting married and I was creating the guest list for the reception. I sat down to write the list under the friends/neighbors/relatives categories. I had writer's block! But

Ask your hostess: "Will you be able to write your list and invite your guests within the next three days?" Let her lead you as to when this can be completed. Within five days of her booking the demonstration, call to see how the guest list is coming if you haven't received it already. This contact is another opportunity to encourage her.

while I was vacuuming the house, or driving my car, I thought of names. Your hostess is the same way. She might sit down right away and put names on paper, but if you give her a couple of days to have it completed, she'll have a more complete list. Additionally, because you'll want her to compose, call, and code the list, she needs to have some time to do this. The urgency of having the list back to you also has a great deal to do with how soon the presentation is. Even if it's four to six weeks away, getting it back quickly is a benefit for both you and the host.

Snail mail was the only way to get a guest list in the "old days." And it is still effective – along with some other alternatives. Many consultants enclose a self-addressed, stamped envelope to make returning the list a simple step. With today's technology, you can suggest she e-mail or fax the list. This is a bit more difficult if you have the nifty guest lists with duplicate copies. The bottom line is that she'll have her list, you'll have yours, and you'll also have a copy for mailing labels (more about this with a *TWIST* in the segment *Paper Potential*).

Within five days of her booking the demonstration, call to see how the guest list is coming if you haven't received it already. This contact is another opportunity to encourage her. If you don't have a list returned within ten days to two weeks, you probably have a hostess with cold feet; her enthusiasm has waned and she'll be glad to get some encouragement from you.

At this point, I use the mail system as a scapegoat. "Mary, your guest list hasn't arrived; I'm wondering if my post office has lost it!" (My apologies if I've offended any postal workers with this statement.) She'll either give you an excuse or a reason why she hasn't completed it. In rare occasions, she has decided to cancel but didn't want to disappoint you, so she decided she'd wait till the day of the presentation. While I abhor cancellations, I'd rather know right away so I can fill my calendar back up.

Reviewing the Guest List
As soon as you get the list, review it. If she has fewer than a dozen people, call her and review the *Top 40 List*. She'll know you care. Remind her that having more people at her demonstration and getting more gifts takes the same amount of time as having just a few guests and getting just a few gifts (more guests, more gifts…see the correlation?).

Has she invited other people on her street? If you don't see any other people listed that live on her street, and she says she doesn't know any of the neighbors, suggest she go high tech – or ask if she minds if you do this simple step for her. Log on at www.msn.com or any other URL that might have the information I'm explaining here. Click on "White Pages." Type in her name and address. If she's listed in the phone book, her name will pop up. Then, near her name, the words "neighbors of" (or something similar) will be listed. Click on those words. Now, you'll have a listing of all her neighbors! You can send a special note with the reminder. You might consider saying this:

> "Lucky You! Your neighbor, _____ (her name), at _____(her address), is hosting a _____ (your company name) demonstration (or party or show or workshop). Stop by and meet some new friends!"

As soon as you get the list, review it. If she has fewer than a dozen people, call her and review the Top 40 List.

Isn't that simple? And, you just never know who her neighbors might be…your next hostess, recruit or leader? She'll love the extra service you provide. I don't explain this step initially because I want to keep the process simple. Only if I don't see neighbors listed do I suggest this. Keep in mind that web sites with this look-up information sometimes change. If you can't see exactly what I've talked about, search the site further.

Check to see if the *Guest List* is in alphabetical order with more than 50 names. I remember the first time I got this huge list and mailed out all the invitations. I was disappointed when only three people showed up. I later found out the host simply went through the church/school/neighborhood directory. She didn't call any of the people nor did she know any of them. Now, there is nothing wrong with her using this as a resource as long as she contacts them, and codes the list. (That's why the code system explained earlier works so well.)

Next, review the names to see if you know any of the people on the list. Some of these might be big fans of yours! Perhaps someone on the list is also someone in your *Business Bank* who has asked you to call this month. Go ahead and call her, get her date in your book, and give your hostess (the one who just mailed the list to you) credit for a booking. Wouldn't that be a fun surprise to tell her you already have a booking for her! Do you think she'll always want to be a hostess of yours? Of course!

If you see names of people you know well and know they collect certain items from your product line, you'll want to bring some of that line to surprise her.

I call the hostess when I receive the list to let her know it's arrived and to thank her for her efforts. At that time, I might ask her to tell me about the guests on the list.

Let me explain why this is so important. It relates to what I mentioned in the *Introduction* about speaking your language. If I had written this book in Portuguese, would you be able to read it? If you live in Brazil or Portugal, you might. Would you go to a demonstration and speak a language the guests didn't know? Of course not. If you plan a demonstration that is geared to, say, children under five and after you've finished, you discover that the host has young children but all the other people are empty nesters, it would be as if you had spoken a foreign language to them. If you get some general demographics of the people she's invited after you get the list, you'll be able to adapt your presentation to their situations. And the guests will love you for paying attention to *their* needs. Of course, sometimes you'll have a cross section of a variety of lifestyles. Remember: every situation is situational.

When I receive the *Guest Lists*, I create a file folder for that host. I write her name on the tab and place her folder in a vertical file that indicates I need to mail out the invitations/reminders. This way, I don't misplace a list.

Remember, names are worth millions! Are you feeling wealthy yet? Keep reading!!

Who Sends the Invitations?

Now that you have this piece of paper—the *Guest List* in your hand—what do you do with it to benefit your hostess and build your business? One question I'm frequently asked is: Who sends the mailing out…the hostess or the consultant? My answer: It depends. However if I could only choose one answer, I'd say the consultant. I'll list my reasons why and then give the situation when I have the hostess take care of this.

First, many people ask: "How do I get my host to give me a list?" The simple answer is positioning the request. Here' a little script:

> "Sydney, one service I provide for all my hosts and customers is that **I send out your printed invitations *after* you contact your friends.** In order for me to do this, of course, I'll need a list from you with everyone's name, address, and phone number. Will you have an opportunity to compose, call, and code a list in the next three days?

[Then you discuss when she can do this.]

"Since your date is on _____ (her date), I'll need to have the list back to me by _____."

The date of her presentation is what establishes the urgency for her to compose, call and code the list so that you can do your part. My belief is "the sooner the better." The best demonstrations are those scheduled and held within a couple of weeks. Therefore, getting the list back quickly is very necessary.

I can already read your mind: "How can I afford to send out 30-to-40 printed invitations when it's 37 cents a piece – that's over $10 plus the cost of the invitations!"

My first response is that you're looking at the cost – rather than an investment in your business. Usually the people who complain about this the most are those who are willing to drop a hundred or more dollars to put a classified ad in a nickel newspaper, hoping that someone will read the ad and then call. Or, will not even think about spending more than that to have a booth at a fair or expo. In both cases, their investment is going to a cold market.

Work to gain the confidence in your business and your presentation abilities, so this mailing becomes an investment in your business. This is your advertising budget, and it's such effective advertising!

With a guest list, you have a hot, targeted, market. The people on the list are friends and acquaintances of your hostess...not just names from a phone book. Direct marketers spend thousands and thousands of dollars to buy lists of names that are targeted, but cold. Then they spend thousands and thousands more to send out mailings that most people throw away! Do you realize what a valuable tool a guest list is and how you are investing practically nothing compared to your potential return? Can you tell I have strong convictions about this? And I haven't even begun to give you other ways to utilize the lists.

When I send out the printed invitations, I am in control. This is my business. I do this everyday. A hostess does not. She might forget to mail them, or not have the money to buy the stamps or the time to prepare and mail them, and so she cancels (of course she gives a different reason for doing so). Some consultants ask the hostess to send the postage (or the cost of the postage) to the consultant. This is TACKY!! It reminds me of a discount grocery store I went to once (did you get the "once" part?). I had to give a deposit to use the cart and then I had to pay for the bags to put my groceries in. The service was non-existent and the prices weren't low enough to exchange for no service. A hostess might agree to this arrangement...once.

Work to gain the confidence in your business and your presentation abilities, so this mailing becomes an investment in your business. This is your advertising budget, and it's such effective advertising! If you have to use a credit card to buy the stamps and then pay the bill after you receive the profits, do so. I remember cutting back on my grocery budget to pay for the stamps (the post office didn't accept credit cards back then). When all was said and done, my grocery budget and over all income increased because I was confident that with my great service, I'd earn many more times the amount of the postage. When you ask a host to assume your responsibility you're conveying, "I don't make enough money doing this, so you'll have to finance my business." Then, you talk about the *great opportunity* you have in the business? This is not congruent.

Now I'll come down off my Lemon Aid Stand to explain when I allow a hostess to hand out the invites herself. For example, when I call to notify her that the list has arrived and she tells me that most of the people work with her, many times she suggests handing out the printed invitations at work. Or, if they are all in her neighborhood, sometimes she suggests taking them around personally. I do allow this at her request; I don't suggest this. Then I call her to be sure she's given them out. Either way, you still have a *Guest List.*

If you elect to do the mailing, do so 10 to 15 days in advance of the demonstration. (Of course, this time frame depends on when she scheduled and when the demonstration is.) This way, people get them 7 to 10 days before the date. It allows for weekends, holidays, and mail delays. In most cases, this is the printed reminder, as you hope that she's already called or visited with her guests to invite them. Mail the hostess one also, so she knows that you've sent them out. On hers, send some more encouraging words.

TWISTS on Mailers

I like to put something different on each mailer – different, but simple. I put a sticker that says "Bring this card/brochure – you could be a wonderful winner." I use address labels to print this message; I don't hand write it. Here are a couple of things you can add:

1. Using a number rubber stamp from an office supply store (this is like a date stamp, but has only numbers), I stamp a number on every piece, most with odd-ending numbers, and just a

couple ending in an even number. I stamp the number right on the sticker telling them to bring the card with them. I like the numbers to be different so if they do compare with other invitees, they don't think I've *rigged* it (even though I have – sort of!). At some point in the presentation, I ask to see who brought their reminder, and then I make a big deal about who has the "Wonderful Number." I simply ask who has a number that ends in an 8 - 6 - 4 - 2 and then I honor the people who have those "even" numbers with a token remembrance – it could be your recruiting materials (isn't that the most valuable information you have?).

2. Another idea is to stamp something seasonal (talk to our direct-sales friends who sell these fun stamps) or use attractive stickers (call The Booster: 1-800-5JENNYB). On these I print a label that says, "Bring this card—match your stamp/sticker—you could be the winner." At the presentation I have a winning stamp/sticker on one of my products. As guests come in, I invite them to see if they *match* the winning sticker on my display. This gets them up to your display right away, looking at your products.

3. Try using *word clues*. For example, put a word describing a particular product on each card. You'll find these words in your product catalog in the description of each item. The winning word is the name of the product. Let me illustrate. I just received my Mary Kay *The Look* from my consultant. She might put a word clue such as these on each card: "exhilarating" "euphoric" "fruity" "floral" "mangosteen" "tart" "banana" "clementine" "velocity". The first eight words are used to describe the fragrance Velocity®. So, Velocity® is the winning word – it's the product. As I ask for people to say the word they have, it leads right into the demonstration and sample of this fragrance.

More people come to the presentation because they are curious, more people are recognized and rewarded, and the most important reason you'll want to do this is the current host and all potential hostesses will see that getting you that Guest List *in a timely manner helps them have a more fun, successful presentation.*

Can you see why you, as the consultant, want to be in charge of mailing out your written reminders? Putting the mailer together is very simple and the activity attached is very easy and so effective. Why? More people come to the presentation because they are curious, more people are recognized and rewarded, and the most important reason you'll want to do this is the current host and all potential hostesses will see that getting you that *Guest List* in a timely manner helps them have a more fun, successful presentation.

Lastly, the task of preparing and mailing these reminders is something you can do on downtime—while you're watching TV, laying out in the sun or waiting to pick up kids from school. Or, better yet, you can pay someone else (like your kids!) to do this for you so you can use your time more wisely to book more shows and recruit and teach new people.

Random Request Calls

Here are even more fun reasons for getting and using a Guest List. A couple of days before her presentation –usually two to three – I make my *Random Request Calls*. I randomly choose a few names off the list – usually one name for every eight to ten on the list. Then I call these people (now you know why I want the phone numbers, and this is another "persuasive point" for the host to get the list back to you). Here's what I say:

> "Jennifer. Christie calling from Northrup Party Plan [you put your name and company in here, of course] – I'm doing the party tomorrow night at Ruth Patterson's home.
>
> (Let her know this connection to the host right away so in her mind she's not thinking 'I've already been invited to a Northrup Party.')
>
> "Of all the many [you want her to feel special!] people Ruth invited, I've selected you to call to see if you have any requests of a particular item for me to bring to the party tomorrow."

This is so incredibly effective! She feels so special! Maybe she's never seen your line before. This gives you a chance to find out about her and her lifestyle. Then you can suggest some things she might want. Or, she might say, "I've been dying to see that itsy bitsy teeny weeny yellow polka dot picture frame…do you have that?" When you demonstrate the requested item at the class, tell everyone to thank Jennifer for requesting you to bring the picture frame. Everyone loves recognition and the feeling of being important. And this is a simple way to do it. And, guess who one of your new bookings will most likely be? You're right…those you called and got to know ahead of time.

Lucky Winner Calls

Here's another similar idea with a Lemon Aid *TWIST*. A few days before the show, I choose a couple of *Lucky Winners*. For every eight to ten people on the list, I call one person. If I see thirty names, I tell myself the lucky numbers today are 16, 20, and 4 (you choose your own numbers). Then I count down the list: 1, 2, 3, 4 – she's a *Lucky Winner*, and so on. The more people on the list, the more people who will be the *Lucky Winners*.

Here's what I say when I dial:

> "Lorraine!! Christie calling from Northrup Parties...I'm doing the show at Diane's this Friday evening! Guess What? Of all the people Diane invited, you have been chosen as one of our Lucky Winners! As soon as you walk in the door, run up to me and say 'I'm a Lucky Winner,' and I'll have something special for you!"

You'll have some dialog here with her, of course. There are also a lot of "what ifs?" One of the biggest is when she says: "Darn, I have bowling that night and I can't come." Then say: "No problem, when you schedule your own show, I'll bring *something special* right to your home! And you can invite all the people you bowl with." Does she jump at this chance to be a host? Not always, but some will accept your offer. Now, if you hadn't done this activity, you wouldn't have met Lorraine at all.

Cut up the Guest List so you have each name/address individually. Put the names in an envelope and take these to the party with you. Use these slips for drawing and recognition.

When the *Lucky Winners* do arrive, award them with something valuable—but not expensive. These people already have a connection with you and are flattered and excited that they were chosen as the *Lucky Winner*. Guess who will be among the first to be your next hostesses? The *Lucky Winners*! It works! It also shows the future hostesses the importance of getting the list to you.

Drawing the Guest List

Here's another way to use the *Guest List* to focus on the guests: Make a photocopy of the list. Cut it up so you have each name/address individually. Put the names in an envelope and take these to the party with you.

Rather than doing drawings where the guests have to fill something out (we know they really don't enjoy extra paper work), simply use these slips of paper for any drawing or recognition. Note: Instead of leaving the names in the paper envelope, (unless you sell paper envelopes) put the slips in one of your products! Or, put each slip inside/on top/next to/or taped to a product on your display table. As guests come in, direct them to the table to find which product you paired them with – a great way to get them looking at your display immediately. When you're ready for the demonstration, have each guest share what they would use the product for. You'll learn quickly who would be a great new consultant. Be ready to guide each person so they will not be embarrassed.

Ask what outfit they would wear the piece of jewelry with.

Plan-Overs for a Feast of New Business

Have you ever prepared a lovely dinner for your family and they ate it all—no leftovers! I love when that happens because clean up is so easy! However, I normally plan meals so I have leftovers (which are really *plan-overs*) and thus, another meal. This process not only saves time in the future, but also allows me to forget about "what's for dinner" for an upcoming day or two.

What does this have to do with using a *Guest List* to build your business? Keep reading. Have you ever gone to a home demonstration and everyone who the host invited came and ordered? This is a rarity in our industry. Normally a third of the people who the host invites will attend, and then another third will usually place an order. From these two groups, you can usually get about three new presentations scheduled. What about the other third of the people who didn't attend or order—the so-called *leftovers*? That's what this suggestion is all about.

You wouldn't leave good food sitting on the table after dinner, nor would you put it down the garbage disposal. However, when you do nothing with the names that are on the guest list whose lives you have not touched, you are throwing names, business, and potential profits away. And more importantly, the people are not being serviced, receiving gifts, or becoming your new friends.

 After a presentation is over, I encourage the hostess to call those who have not attended or ordered to see if they want something (for a *TWIST* on encouraging additional orders see the *Paper Potential* segment of this book). Sometimes the hostess will even encourage them to book a demonstration if she is working for a goal and needs it. Do all hostesses call back all people? Of course not! But you can – if you have the *Guest List* with the phone numbers.

 What do you say? It's very simple:

> "Cathy! Christie calling from Northrup Parties. I missed meeting you at Merrilee's last night."
> She'll proceed to tell you why she didn't come. She might even say, "I hate home parties." Or, "I have so many of your products, I just don't need any more."
>
> Let her do this so you can access her temperature about your company and product. If this is the case (which it will be often—they don't like/want/need your product), just listen. *Don't try to overcome her objection.* She might tell

16

you she had other commitments, she was too tired, etc. etc. etc...

Whatever she says, simply reply: "Since you were unable to join us, I'm calling to invite you to be a hostess with me." Then...listen. If she says a flat out NO!, simply tell her you hope to meet her in the future. Be very nice and happy. Never appear disappointed.

On the other hand, she might say YES! More often than not, her schedule prevented her attendance. Because I personally contact her, I discover a better time or season for me to connect with her in the future, and then I follow through appropriately. In other words, these "names on a paper" now become real people—and future profits to all involved. Believe it or not, I scheduled many a demonstration by calling these *plan-overs* back. Sometimes, they were better than the original *meal* (demonstration). Names truly are worth millions...millions of new bookings, referrals, sales, and mostly millions of new friends! For more information on keeping track of these contacts and when to connect with them, refer to *The Lemon Aid Deed Alphabet*, pages 18 – 20 where I discuss a *Business Bank*.

I hope your goal is to have hostesses for life.

I have shared many ways that a *Guest List* can benefit you, your hostesses, and your guests. Remember, all of your are working on the same team. One does not lose while the others profit. It's a three-way win: the guests have special attention; you sell, book and recruit more; and your hostess has a better turn out with more fun and more gifts. And there is still one other way all three parties involved benefit; this shows up months (hopefully) and maybe even years later.

Hostesses for Life

I hope your goal is to have hostesses for life, meaning whenever a hostess schedules with you and you do your presentation, she is so loyal she would never think of having another consultant from your company except you—unless, of course, she joins your team (which shows true loyalty)! One way to insure this is to give extra service and that's where a guest list comes in.

As I share these concepts around the country, I receive a great many questions from the Lemon Aid Learners. One is the fear that the hostess will not want to take the time to collect her friends' addresses and phone numbers. However, when she sees that you are using some of the tips I've already shared, she'll see the value to her and to her guests, and she won't question your suggestions.

Also, when you capture the information once, you'll not have to obtain it again – even though your hostess will have many, many more parties with you.

You do this by holding on to each *Guest List* and keeping them in a safe place. My suggestion is a simple file folder as mentioned earlier—one for each hostess. In this folder, I put everything pertaining to that hostess: including her guest list, order forms, etc.. In about six months, I'll call her to see if she is ready to have another demonstration with me. When she excitedly agrees, I can speed things up. I have her guest list in front of me; she can start at step two rather than step one. I let her know I have her guest list already and then say: "All we need to do is update and add to the list." I cannot tell you how surprised my hostesses were when they knew I kept their information. Remember, names are worth MILLIONS. Now you have millions of compliments from happy hostesses, and you'll have MILLIONS more new bookings because they know when they are your hostess, you make having a presentation easy for them—so they'll do more presentations. They love the extra service, and might even call you to get a list of family and friends when they prepare their Christmas card list!

Additionally, when you review the *Guest List*, which can simply be done over the phone, you are also updating your customer data base. For example, as you read off the names, your hostess will let you know who has moved and will give you the new address, if she has it. Plus, you can assure her that even if her friends have moved out of the area, you can still send a catalog to them (at your expense; after all you'll benefit greatly) in their new town. Who knows, maybe that person will join your team because she might not have a consultant from your company in her new city.

You can also find out other information about your customers because as you review the list, your current host will tell you about new babies, weddings, even deaths and divorces. This personal touch really builds your business. Companies, including mine, spend many hours updating customer data. Your hostess can be your assistant in helping you manage and build your client files – all while she's having fun and earning great gifts from you!

Guest Lists Can Save a Show
Now, allow me to share a personal experience where the *Guest List* literally "saved" the show. A hostess of mine had a *Sour Situation* and had no choice but to cancel her show. I can't remember exactly why, but it was something devastating like an illness or death of a

relative. She called me in a panic; she did not have the time or energy to call all the people she knew would show up at her home. She also didn't want everyone to drive to her home just to find a note hanging on the door.

When she called, I assured her everything would be taken care of. I quickly pulled out her *Guest List* and called everyone. Yes, I left many voice mail messages. And for the ones I connected with, I was able to get orders for things they had planned on buying as well as to schedule more demonstrations. After all, when the guests saw that I was so willing to help their friend, they knew I would also service them well.

When a hostess advances to become a consultant, you have a file of all her former guests. This gives her a boost as she begins to build her own customer base.

In the end, in spite of her personal *Sour Situation* I was able to do the *TWIST* and she still ended up having a successful party with many gifts. She became a *Hostess for Life* because we had a back-up plan – we had worked together to create a valuable guest list, which ended up paying dividends for everyone involved: hostess, guests, and consultant. This is truly a perfect way to build people as you build your business.

Segment Two

Packaging

What product do you sell? Is it baskets to decorate homes? Top-quality papers and albums to preserve memories for generations? Do you sell air-tight food storage containers? Maybe your product is jewelry, clothing, or skin care products. Are you marketing wall and home décor items? Whatever the product, the bottom line is you're teaching people how to have better packaging for what they value most. Be it packaging for their photos, holders for candles, nutritional supplements for their healthy body, or creative ways to design and stamp greeting cards and scrap book pages. Everything comes back to how we present something we own and value. And, we want that presentation to be pleasant and attractive.

When guests arrive at the home presentation, the first thing they see is your *personal packaging*, next your *product packaging*, and lastly your *paper packaging*.

Personal Packaging

You know you're an excellent demonstrator. You are filled with ideas and tips and are eager to share them with the world—if only the world would want to hear them. Gee, you'd even settle for your next-door neighbor to listen. One question I often ask my consulting clients when they confess to needed more bookings, is "What is your *Personal Packaging* like?" This sounds like an elementary question. After all, we've been taught proper personal grooming. Everyone showers daily, wears deodorant, and has clean clothes, hair, and shoes. Or, do they? Not necessarily.

In the introduction to this book, I shared my first home party experience as a guest. One of the things that distracted me the most was the *Personal Packaging* of the demonstrator. That image has been with me for over 20 years. What do people remember about your *Personal Packaging*? Now, before you go out and purchase designer suits, let's talk…

Let me say up front I'm not advocating the business suit as a standard for the industry. What you wear depends on what you're demonstrating. For example, if you're doing a rubber stamp workshop, wearing a dry-clean only suit would simply not make sense! If you sell toys, getting down on the floor in a dress and heels would be very awkward. Likewise, if you're selling items related to personal dress and image (clothing, jewelry, makeup and skin care), you need to be a product of your product and dress up—not appear in jeans or sweats. If you're demonstrating food preparation, don't wear clothing with fragile fabrics that can be ruined with tomato sauce or grape juice! In other words, dress for the occasion, but dress a notch above what you anticipate the guests will be wearing.

Most likely you'll be wearing your company's name tag. However, when guests arrive at the party, you should stick out like a proud, professional person so that they know at a glance you are the demonstrator. Here's an example: Quite frankly, I've been disappointed at the dress of teachers in public schools in the past years. They tend to dress to the level of the students. By doing this, they are not getting the respect they deserve because they are becoming "one of them," rather than establishing themselves as the leader of the class. I realize this is not true in all cases; I've just witnessed a trend in my local schools.

Dress a notch above what you anticipate the guests will be wearing. When guests arrive at the party, you should stick out like a proud professional so that they know at a glance you are the demonstrator.

When you board an airplane, you're greeted by the flight crew. And they're all dressed in the company uniform. In some companies, the "uniform" is polished and professional; in others, casual shorts are the order. Either way, you know who the crew is. If you boarded a plane and the captain and flight attendants were in sweats, T-shirts, and baseball caps, would you have as much confidence in them? I think not. Our dress speaks volumes about our intentions to serve. If we care about our personal selves, we'll care about serving our customers.

For three years, my business was based in the Detroit, Michigan area—you know, "the Automobile Capital of the World." Many of my classes were hosted and attended by executives from these companies. At these demonstrations, I wanted to dress at a level a notch above them. However, I also did many outside park parties. I knew my customers at these events would be wearing cute short shorts and skimpy tops. While I didn't wear the same types of clothes as I would with the car executives, I wore more casual attire, but always planned a notch above what I anticipated my guests would be wearing.

As a professional speaker, I once went against my own wisdom on the dressing issue: I had done several presentations for a particular company, and noticed that most of the ladies wore slacks and nice pantsuits. Since I believe in dressing a "notch above," I normally wear a dress or suit when I speak (I'm a big fan of Weekenders®

Clothing!). But on this occasion, my presentation was on a Saturday morning. I'd be finished by lunch, and then I had a four-hour drive to the next city. I needed to be comfortable. So, I decided I'd dress like (instead of a notch above) what I'd seen the company's consultants wear in the past. I donned a nice pant suit. But when I got to the meeting, most of the ladies were in business suits with skirts and jackets. I was a little—no, a lot—embarrassed! From then on, I've heeded my own advice. Dress a notch above what you anticipate your guests wearing!

Many of the guests at our classes come straight from work. They're in business dress, and when they see some of us dressed inappropriately, they perceive that we are just visiting, that our business really isn't that important to us. That's why many people outside of the direct sales industry tell us to "go get a real job."

One last *test for dress* is to pretend you are dressing for a job interview—because you are! You're hoping that everyone will say to you: "I want to hire you to come to my house and teach my friends how to..." Although our clothes don't actually "talk," how we dress speaks volumes!

Product Packaging

We're not a retail store, but to our customers and hostesses, we are a store. Therefore, keeping our products in tip-top shape for a demonstration is very important. Look at the items in your sales kit. Are they "display material?" By this, I mean, would they be nice enough to put in the store window? Or, are they soiled, scratched, dented, or damaged? Remember the story in the introduction about the demonstrator taking spaghetti out of the bowl so she could bring it to the party? I'm an advocate for having one product for your kit and another for personal use. I don't know of any law that says you can only buy one of an item. When we use the same items at our shows that we use in our homes, we're conveying *it's not important to have more than one of these.* Yet, we teach our customers (or at least we should be teaching them) that they can "buy one for the bath, one for the kitchen, and one for the bedroom."

I've been embarrassed at presentations when I left something home because I was using it for myself and then didn't have the item to demonstrate. I lost out on sales and on bookings. You're probably thinking, "But I don't need two of the same wall hanging in my home." Exactly my point! You might not need it in your home, but you need it for your business.

Let me give you an illustration with a *TWIST*. When we purchased our current home, we toured two or three model homes in the area. These homes were lavishly furnished! The decorations helped us to want to buy the house so we could live in something just like the model. Now, did the builder of the development bring his own couches, chairs, dishes, and wall hangings into the model homes? Of course not! The items were purchased solely for the use of decorating the model home. After all the homes were sold, and before the new owners moved into the model homes, the builder had a sale! That's right! Everyone in the neighborhood was notified that the decorations were for sale, and marked down to below reasonable prices. After all, they were considered *used* even though they had only been *viewed.*

Before you leave your house, look in the mirror and ask: "Would I hire me?"

How does this relate to your business? At the end of each season or catalog, have an exclusive event. I'd invite hostesses only. (And wouldn't this would be another excellent reason to be a hostess?) Now, they can come to your home and purchase your "viewed" items at a marked down price. Then, you take the money made from the sale and invest it in more products for your business—not to go out to dinner or on vacation. This way, you'll always have the newest items for showing and selling! And, they'll all be in perfect, presentable shape.

I realize some of you do *hands-on* demonstrations, actually using products such as kitchen tools, ink pads, scissors, stamps, etc. You can still keep these looking nice and updated. For instance, if a certain bowl goes through a color change and is not available in the older color you have, don't show the old color at all! Never say, "You used to be able to get this bowl in blue like I have here. Now it only comes in red like you see in the catalog." Sure enough, people will want the blue one! But that's not the point I'm trying to make. Rather, you're conveying to people that you don't see the value in keeping the newest colors in your kit, so why would they want the newest in their kitchen?

Paper Packaging

When your guests come to your demonstration, they'll know right away you're a professional because of your *Personal Packaging.* And as they look at your display, they'll see and feel a *professionally cared-for display of products.* At some point in the demonstration, you'll distribute catalogs, order forms, and recruiting and booking literature. *Is your paper work polished?*

To illustrate: Have you ever gone to a restaurant and been handed a menu that looked like somebody ate their lunch off of it? I have. And I didn't want to touch the thing—let alone eat at that restaurant (I also won't eat at a food establishment with filthy floors and dirty restrooms—another example of packaging). When you hand a customer a product catalog, what will her impression be of your business? Does the catalog look like hundreds of people have thumbed through it while eating party refreshments? Or will she feel it's a special gift to her?

I realize some party plan companies have a catalog that is more than a sales tool. Many are reference manuals that people actually purchase. Therefore, more than one person might use a catalog or reference manual at a demonstration. However, frequent attendees should be encouraged to bring their "manuals" to every event. This reduces how many people will "borrow" a catalog from you as most will be owners. Refer to the segment on *Paper Potential* for ideas on having guests recycle their catalogs.

For other companies, I suggest creating "master catalogs." I used this for years and have seen a trend toward this at many home parties. Simply put the individual pages of a catalog in plastic page protectors and then put the protectors in a folder or binder. Guests use these binders to order; if they want a personal catalog to take home, they either purchase one (if that's your company's policy), or you give them one (more ideas on this under *Paper Potential*). This idea works for the 8 ½ x 11 inch catalogs as that is the size the page protectors come in. Some binders/folders have inside pockets to put other literature like recruiting brochures, party planning information, flyers listing specials, and so forth. You can even attach a pen to the catalog with a string. The only liability here is some people think they get to take the binders home. I simply tease them and ask them to leave the binders with me—I let them take home a "cousin" to my binder. Contact the Booster at 1-800-5-JENNYB and ask about guest folders.

Now that I've shared this easy idea, think of the restaurants that have their menus coated in plastic – they can easily clean and reuse them. Those who offer only paper menus put up with dirty, soiled literature and eventually throw a lot of them away. The choice is yours: paper or plastic?

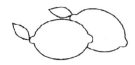

Segment Three
Meet and Greet

For just a few moments, please think like a guest at a home party. You walk into the room where the display is. What does the demonstrator do? Is she sitting on a chair next to the display table "guarding" her products? Does she have her back to you because she's still setting up? Or, does she come over to you and greet you? Which action would make you feel the most welcome? Now switch to your consultant mode. How do you welcome people at your classes? Have you ever considered that the way you welcome—or ignore—guests as they arrive sets the tone for their deciding if they will or will not "hire" you to come to their home or office? Let me give some ways to *meet and greet* and then create a setting for new hostesses in your schedule.

The price of establishing relationships is paying attention to people.

Remember…people first, product second. If you are still setting up as people are arriving, stop to *meet and greet* the guests. People are more apt to buy from you when you pay attention to them. That last line might read as if your only goal is to make money. Instead, please read it with the idea of what the price of establishing relationships is: paying attention. Your total focus should be on the people.

As you walk toward the guests, extend your hand. You are giving the non-verbal cue that says "Come, join my circle of friends." As you extend your hand, she extends hers and you share a hand shake. Now, some women shy away from shaking hands. If you feel hesitancy, drop your hand. Don't let anyone feel uncomfortable. Sometimes a touch on the forearm is a good way to connect. When you connect with people physically, it's easier to connect emotionally. And, as you get to know a group well, they'll run up and hug you when you meet! Let's continue... As you shake her hand, you say:

"Welcome to the Party! I'm your _____ (company name) consultant, Christie. And you are?"

Allow her to "fill in the blank." This is a softer approach. As she says her name, let it sink into your mind. If it's a name that is not familiar, repeat it and even ask her to say it again. For example, I have a good friend from Finland. Her name is Pirjo (peer-yo), a name I'd never heard before. The only way I could remember it was by repeating it back several times and asking how to spell her name. (In just a bit, I'll give you many more hints to remember names). If her name is one that can be spelled several different ways (like "Christie"), I ask, "Is that Kelly with a "y" or an "ie" on the end?" Or, "Is that Karen with a "K" or a "C?" I'm letting her know that not only do I want to know her name, I want to be sure I spell it correctly.

The next question I ask is: "And how do you know our hostess tonight?"

I'm finding out information about her as she explains they've known each other since kindergarten, they work together, they are sisters, etc. I begin to know more about the guests as I know the connection she has with my hostess. And then that question leads to others. "Wow, since kindergarten, what city did you live in then?" And when you know about a person, you remember her and you remember important things about her…like her name! When you show an interest in other people, they think you are the most interesting person! And, they want to be around you more often. So, what do they do? Book a Show!!

Segment Four

The Name Game

In the last segment, I shared ideas of initially meeting and greeting your guests. Let's take this to the next level and discover how we'll remember their names. I can already hear you say, "I can't remember names." Well, you're right. You can't. Only read this next section if you really want to remember names. And tell yourself that you can do anything you want to—even remember names!

As you're meeting and greeting *the guests and learning their names, you want them to have something with their name on it in their hand.*

As I'm *meeting and greeting* the guests and learning their names, I hand each of them something: a catalog, an order form, or a *Getting to Know More About You* form. These are discussed at length in the *Paper Potential* segment of this book. You decide what you're going to hand her at this moment. I just want her to have something with her name on it in her hand.. That's what I said....something with her name on it. So, as she tells me her name is Teresa, I ask, "Is that Teresa with a 'Th' or just a 'T'"? Now, as I'm "inking, not just thinking", I'm remembering her name!! Remember more on this in the *Paper Potential* segment.

Alphabet Association

What are some other ways for you to remember your guests' names? I know a lot of us in the party plan industry have used the "Alphabet Association." We have everyone go around the room, tell their first name and then using the first letter in their first name, they are to tell everyone something like: where they'd like to go on vacation, what's their favorite color, what kind of car they want to drive, etc. For example, I'd say, "I'm Christie, I'm going to the Caribbean in a Cherry-Colored Corvette." Now, really sharp consultants (and I've been at their demonstrations) will have the guest relate it to the product. For example: "I'm Christie, my favorite product is the Chopper." Or: "I'm Christie, I want to do a scrap book page from my camping trip." This is fun and even gets funny. Well, let's do a *TWIST* with some ideas you probably haven't seen, heard, or used.

Cheat Sheet

After everyone has a place to sit and is seated, I ask, "Ladies, you know how when you go to a wedding you get to sign the guest register book? Well, I want to remember all of you being at tonight's party, so will you please autograph my guest register tonight?"

27

Now, what is this *guest register*? Well, once again I'll refer you to the *Paper Potential* segment of this book for numerous ways to use this. But in this section, I'll tell you what it is and how it will help you in remembering guests' names.

The *guest register* can be as simple as a lined notebook with paper. Or, you can photo copy the one I've created in the back of this book, put it in a binder and decorate it. What I really prefer is to buy pretty journals with ring binding. This way the book will lie flat, and it's pretty. As you'll notice from the sample, I just want the person's name, address, and phone number. That's it. If you're using the journal or lined paper, simply write column headings: Name – Phone – Address. And pass the book around.

Now, one of my pet peeves when I go to home parties is that I have to write my name, phone, and address so many times I get writer's cramp! You know what I mean—the *order form*, the *door prize drawing*, etc. That's why I suggested writing the person's name on the order form or "*Getting to Know More About You* card." Again, these will be discussed in detail in the, you guessed it—*Paper Potential* Segment. I only want my guests to have to write their name, address, and phone number one time. So, keep it simple. If I have only one choice of where I want this information, this guest register is the place.

The *guest register* is passed around the room in the order (hint, hint) of where they are seated. Now, the register comes back to me. I remember Donna because she has such a bright pink sweater on. And I know that Carolyn is two people down from Donna. But, I cannot remember the person in between these two ladies. Now, don't be embarrassed to be reminded of someone's name. You are only conveying that you are eager to remember her name. But, this cheat sheet will eliminate that. Casually glance down at the *guest register*. Remember, you know Donna and on the other side is Carolyn. So, look and see whose name is in between the two. Remember, this guest register was passed around in the order of their seating—which is why I wait to pass it around! Voilá, I see Juliet's name. Now I can call her by name as I ask her, "Juliet, what is your favorite item on the table...?"

Use It so You Don't Lose It

That's the next way to remember names. Use the names over and over. People never get tired of hearing their own name—unless their name is "mom"! And the more you say a person's name the more you remember…and the more impressed your guests are. And guess what? The more bookings you get!

Put It in LIGHTS

Yes, we love to hear our name. Just think how it would feel to SEE your name in lights! Or, at least on a poster or a sign. Here's another fun *TWIST* where you'll be focusing on your guests. Now, before you can do this fun recognition, you have to have a guest list ahead of time from your hostess (See Segment One – *Pre-Presentation*). Randomly select one lucky number. Sometimes this will be the "middle" person. If I have 30 on a list, I choose number 15. It's all up to you!

If I have only one choice of where to capture a person's name, address, and phone number, the Guest Register is the place.

Of course, you can also do a *TWIST*. Perhaps you can consult with your hostess and ask if there is someone she knows will be attending who might need some extra recognition. Remember the *Top 40 List*? One of the categories I write is "Anyone who is going through a difficult time." This could be someone with an illness, no job, or other *Sour Situation*. This might be just the person to recognize.

Before I go to the party, I make a poster or sign and decorate it with markers, rubber stamps, and stickers (use your product if this is what you sell!). On this poster I write: Congrats to our Lemon Aid Learner of the Day: Cathy Vickers. Obviously, you're not going to write "Lemon Aid Learner" (that's what I call our "Guest of the Day" at my live Learning Adventures™); you'll do the *TWIST*. If you sell decorating items you'll say, "Decorator of the Day." If your company deals with food and related products, it can be "Cook of the Day." These are simple *TWISTS*. Use your own creativity for something fun.

Now, when Cathy walks in…what does she see? (Just a note: check with the hostess to be sure Cathy is planning on attending. Sometimes I actually wait to write her name until she arrives. Then I discreetly finish the poster and hang it up. If Cathy hasn't arrived by the time I'm ready to get started, I can quickly choose someone else.) She sees her name in "lights!" What is she going to think? She usually doesn't say anything. Somewhere in the demonstration, you'll say "We have a special guest with us tonight, it's our Basket Buddy of the Day; Cathy come on down." I reward her with something inexpensive—but valuable. Then I tell everyone in the room they can autograph her poster and that Cathy gets to take the poster home with her if she wants; all my featured guests take this! You can also take a picture of her by the poster. This is another way of recognizing a guest, and also remembering her name. I bet she'll always remember you; more about that later.

Another poster/name idea (remember, you're not going to use all these ideas at every class!): Have a poster prepared that reads, "Welcome Beauty Queens" (that's an idea if you sell cosmetics, skin care, clothing, lingerie, or jewelry items). Around these words, have everyone sign their name and how they know the hostess. For example, "Lisa Young, Neighbor" As the guests sign the poster, they see who else is at the show and conversations flow! Additionally, you can see the poster, remember the names, and know how the guests know the hostess. Afterwards, the hostess has a fun *piece of art* to remember the demonstration.

Or, you can use the Guest List (can you see why I'm so passionate about the list?) and print each name on the poster. When people arrive, they write how they know the hostess next to their name. Or, they can write down how many miles they drove to come to the party. Maybe you'll have them write down the state they were born in…there are lots of directions you can take. This activity gets people mixing, mingling, communicating, and connecting—that's what makes the class fun! And they like you right away because you've just recognized them by putting their name in "lights." The by-product of this activity is you get accustomed to the names as you prepare the poster…then all you're doing is matching the names to the faces. You also find out more information about each guest. This not only helps in remembering names but also recognizes each individual.

Just Say "No" to Name Tags

Are you wondering why I haven't used the *obvious* technique most people use to remember the names of others? That's because I don't believe in the obvious—name tags—to remember names. They are fine if you want to read—not remember—names. Another reason is that you're looking at the wrong part of their anatomy! I want to look at their eyes. I don't want to look at their chest. I might get jealous! So, I just look in their eyes and I concentrate and remember things about them.

The Name to Remember

I'm going to give you a test now. This is an *easy* test. Think back to a time you attended a home party *as a guest,* and the party you attended was from a company other than the one you sell for right now. I'm going to give you a few other stipulations. The demonstrator who presented is someone you don't know, so it can't be a relative. or friend. And you can't have held a demonstration with her - either with your company or with her company. In fact, you only met this person one time. Now, what company are you thinking of? Who was the demonstrator? Over 95% of the people cannot name him/her. The percentage who do remember the consultant do so because they remember her exceptional service… or her exceptionally poor service.

What if you needed more of the product from this company and you didn't know any other consultants in that company; how would you contact this person? It would be extremely difficult if you didn't even know her name!

Let's do another test. Pretend you go to a party where you bought a gorgeous serving bowl. Your neighbor, Denise, was the hostess. Her friend from work, Lynette, was the consultant (are you following me here?). Your sister, Diane, comes by to visit; she sees the bowl and wants one for herself. Who do you tell her to contact? Most will say, "I got it from my friend, Denise." You see, most people tend to associate their purchase with the hostess rather than the consultant. Which name do you want your customers to remember?

Most people tend to associate their purchase with the hostess rather than the consultant. Which name do you want your customers to remember?

It's time to do the *TWIST*…we've just remembered the names of all the guests at the show. The next goal is to get them to remember *your* name so anytime your company is mentioned, your name automatically pops up in their minds. It seems it should be rather easy; after all, you've remembered ten or more names. But unless you tell them to remember you, they probably won't. Read on…

Let Your Guests "Ink" You

I suggested that when you met and greeted your guests, you write their names on their order forms. Let's do a *TWIST*….when you get to the part of your demonstration where you briefly explain the order form, have everyone write your name and phone number on their order form in the consultant/representative box. If you have carbonless order forms, it goes through all copies. So, not only do you have the guests "ink, not just think" your name, you also don't have to stamp all the copies with your name!

Make It Permanent—In the Planner

You know how I used to break the ice at the beginning of a party? I would very seriously ask, "Okay ladies, how many came tonight thinking about having a _____ party?" Of course, most everyone would look at me a bit defensively. I could tell they were thinking: "This thing is just getting started and already she's putting the pressure on!" But then I would break into a huge smile and say, "Alright, come on, 'fess up. I know a lot of you have been *thinking* 'Boy, I'm not going do one of those _____ parties; she better not ask me!' See, you were 'thinking' about it...you were 'thinking' you don't want to date a party, right?"

At that point, many burst out laughing with me. Did I only break the ice? No. Because, along with the ice, I broke down *barriers*. Barriers thrown up that would prevent me from dating parities. Because I told them "I know how you feel. I'm not going to force anybody to do anything they don't want to." That was one of the best ways I found to win hostesses as I influenced many people.

After that, I asked the ladies right up front:

> "How many of you here brought your planner or calendar?" Hands would go up, and they would start showing their PDAs and other gadgets. I continued: "Great! If you brought your planner, pull it out and turn to the address book. Whenever you want to contact me, turn to the "L" section of your book."

Now, you might be wondering why I said "L" when my name is Christie, which begins with a "C."

Here's why: If you're a consultant for Longaberger®, what letter would you have your guests list your name under? I hope you said "B" for baskets because that's how people classify Longaberger, even though the line includes pottery and other accessories. People classify you under the category of baskets. Most don't even know how to spell the company name – they might think it's "Lotsaberger!"

Another example features a candle company, PartyLite® that everyone can learn from. Consultants from this company should have their guests turn to the "C", rather than "P." Why? Because people think of product classification first, company name second. A PartyLite consultant at one of my classes shared an experience to drive home this point. One of her hostesses was puzzled because her next-door neighbor, a candle lover, didn't come to her party. She called the neighbor the next day and said: "I missed you at my PartyLite party. You told me you loved candles." The neighbor said, "Candles? I thought PartyLite was a low fat cooking class; I've already been to enough of those!" Isn't that interesting? Most people remember product category first, company name second.

Now, let's go back to the planner: Why do I want you to put my phone number and name under "L" when my name starts with "C." It's the *Category*…you think of Lemons before you think of Christie when you want new ideas for your business. Here's and important T-I-P: When I announce my phone number for the audience to put it in their address book, I say my phone number s-l-o-w-l-y. Now, you know who's got their planners with them. So you say:

> "Now before you put your calendars away, feel free to look at your schedule and when you want to have your own show; I'll check to see if I have that day available." Isn't that a subtle dating hint? You know what they do…they laugh! I just teased them about "thinking" about having a party, and now I'm teasing them again. They laugh. And when people laugh, they listen!

Most people think of product classification first, company name second.

For those guests who do not have a planner with them, this is what I say:

> "If you don't have your address book with you, when you get home tonight make sure you go to your personal address book, or even the phone book…open up to the letter "L" for Lemon Aid Lady (you'll put the first letter of the category you represent) because when you need me, I'll be there…if you remember who I am."

Activity to Remember

Do you want some tips on how to have people actively remember your name? Have them do something really fun so they'll associate the action with who you are. When you experience this class, Presentations for Profit$ in a live Learning Adventure™ setting, you'll do an exercise that will help you always remember what you learned. In the meantime, let me give you some ideas. If you are a consultant with Tupperware®, have everyone pretend to hold on to a bowl, walk their fingers around the rim, and while they're doing this repeat exactly what you're going to say: "My name is _____ (fill in the blank with *your name* so they are repeating *your name*.)" If you sell jewelry, have them pretend they are putting a ring on their finger, earrings on their ears, or a necklace on their neck and repeat, "My name is _____ (fill in the blank with *your name* so they are repeating *your name* –not their own.)" This is a fun, crazy way for people to associate you with your product and an activity that connects you with the product. As they do this, you can also make up a poem or a jingle.

Personal Icon

I've saved the best way to keep you in the minds of your customers to the last. Imagine yourself driving down the road and you come to an intersection. On your right side you see a red, hexagon-shaped sign. No words, just a sign. What do you automatically do? The correct answer is STOP. I hope that's what you do!

Here's another example: You arrive at home and turn on your computer. You want to finish a letter you've been writing. On the desk top of your computer you see a picture of a file folder—no words—just a picture of a file folder. You click on the file folder picture and now you see a listing of all the files you've saved.

In these two examples, the red hexagon sign and the file folder are called icons. Icons are images that represent something. When we see the image, we identify with the thoughts and actions the icon represents. Let me give you another example...

After finishing the letter on your computer, you drive to the grocery store. As you go through the frozen food section, you see cans of frozen lemonade concentrate. What is going to come to your mind? What will you remember as you look at that lemonade? If you're thirsty, you're probably imagining how the cold drink will feel on your parched throat. If you're "thirsty" for more bookings, I hope the lemonade will remind you of what you've learned in this book written by the Lemon Aid Lady™. And, as you remember the tips, you'll begin implementing them.

In other words, my goal of having the Lemon Aid Lady™ as my personal icon is to help you remember what I've taught you. And when you remember what I've taught you, you remember me—not my real name, but my personal icon. So, when you're "thirsty" for more ideas, or when you meet other "thirsty" people, you'll easily recall how to get in touch with me: www.lemonaidlady.com. Most people remember my personal icon, The Lemon Aid Lady™, and sometimes never know my name. That's okay; that's the best way.

One of my clients did a presentation to a company meeting using some of the concepts from my book, *Totally Terrific Team Themes*. She showed the book and told the audience it was written by Christie Northrup. Another of my clients was at the meeting. She wanted a copy of the book and called the number the presenter gave. She was so surprised to learn that my name and my personal icon were one in the same. Had the presenter simply used my personal icon, rather than my name, the second client would have simply gone to my website—which has the same name as my personal icon, www.lemonaidlady.com

Think of this: A woman attends one of your home parties. She purchases a bottle of bubble bath from you. Now, every time she uses this, does she remember your name? Probably not. (Although I do hope you have placed a sticker with your contact information on the bottom of her bubble bath bottle!) So, how can you position yourself in her mind so that she never forgets you, and in fact, remembers your personal icon so well that she actually tells other people about you?

Personal icons position you to be *different from everybody else in your company and in your category*. In marketing, the three ways to get people to remember you are: 1. *Be the first to do something.* Most Americans know that George Washington was the first president of the United States. Who was the second president? 2. *Be the Best at what you do.* I'd guess that even if Americans didn't know who the first president of the country was, they know that Michael Jordan is a great basketball player—he's the best! People remember him!

You may be thinking: "I'm not the first or the best...so what do I do?" The third way to get yourself in people's minds is to *be different*—this you can do by using a *personal icon*!

Your customers might describe you as, "Oh, she's my basket lady." That's good, but are you the only "basket lady"? No, there are thousands more, and more than one company sells baskets! So, what can you do to set yourself apart? Create your own *personal icon*; there are several ways to do this.

Picture the Icon

An icon is normally an everyday object. When a person sees this object, an image pops up in her mind. I've had clients use different foods or candy for their icon. One lady, whose name was Mary and sold make up, used M&M® candy and told her guests to remember Make up Mary (M&M), then reminded everyone they could Make Money—another play on the M&M. One woman in the Chicago area chose a gold nugget as her personal icon and handed out "treasure" candy pieces as she explained that her service was worth gold and her customers were a treasure to her.

How can you position yourself in her mind so that she never forgets you, and in fact, remembers your personal icon so well that she actually tells other people about you?

Name is the Icon

Although names don't always conjure a picture in people's minds, they can create a non-visual personal icon. My doctor's name is Kerry Perry—it rhymes. When I think of doctor, I think of her first. A consultant at one of my classes name is Sheri Perry. Because our industry is based on sharing, she did some creative *TWISTS* on her name.

Even though I use a lemon for my personal icon, I could also use my name as an icon. I love the Christmas holidays and can tell people that having a demonstration with me is like "Christiemas" at the "Northrup" Pole! Promoting this personal icon is endless! Look at your name—maybe you have a middle name or initial that no one knows about. Do your initials spell a word? My maiden name is Anderson; my initials spell CAN. I could do another personal icon with these initials…CAN you? Can you do a little play on your name? Does your name have rhyme and/or rhythm to it—like Ruthie Robins or Camilla Curtis?

Is your name actually an item? I had a friend years ago named Candy Krane. What comes to your mind when you hear that? You're right; she handed out candy cane pens to her guests at her demonstrations. Everyone remembered Candy!

What if you don't have a name like what I've mentioned? Keep reading and *TWISTING!*

Something Unique about You

A woman who is a consultant for a candle company was at one of my live Learning Adventures. She had a difficult time grasping this concept, then all of a sudden I saw the "candle glow" in her eyes as she did a mental *TWIST*. She said, "I was born on the Fourth of July, and since I sell candles, I can use the firecracker as my personal icon and relate it to candles."

Experience Your Icon

This is actually how I created my personal icon of the Lemon Aid Lady™. Our family had gone through a very sour experience with a business we owned. Throughout those trying times, I could feel myself becoming very bitter. I remember telling my husband that we had a choice to keep getting bitter or we could make things better—it was up to us.

I eventually thought about the lemon. Initially, lemon juice is very sour and bitter. However, when the juice is added to something else—like sugar and water—it becomes sweet and tasty. I knew that having a *Sour Situation* was actually the seed of future *Sweet Successes and Juicy Profits.* Had that experience not been sour, I would not be the Lemon Aid Lady today, and you wouldn't be learning these new ideas.

Developing my personal icon took several years. It's still being perfected as will your own personal icon. Don't worry if the idea doesn't just enter your mind right now. But if something does come to you right away, start playing with it.

Product

A good friend, who is a leader with Princess House®, wanted people to remember that she's like Mary Poppins who brings in a bag of fun products—she calls herself the Poppins Party Girl. Because one of the flagship products of her company is a glass cake plate, Cathy ties those two ideas together with a Mary Poppins-esque saying: Her business card reads, "Every task you undertake becomes a piece of cake!" A great slogan and recruiting line!

Do you have a product that is a standard in your line, such as the Princess House® cake plate? How will customers remember you because of this product? Cathy re-named herself the Poppins Party Girl and tied in part of a song with her slogan.

E-Mail

Look at your e-mail address. By the way, since you're in business, I hope you have your own e-mail account and aren't sharing one with your spouse and/or kids. With free e-mail services like yahoo and hot mail, set up your own. This way, you won't have to worry that someone else deletes important messages. And, you can create an e-mail address that relates to your personal icon.

When I was in Phoenix, Arizona and taught this class, one of the Lemon Aid Learners was trying to develop her personal icon. When I mentioned the e-mail address, she immediately discovered her icon. She is a consultant with PartyLite Candles. Her e-mail address is TheWickChick—appropriate for candles. The class was in February, just as the Easter items were hitting the stores. So Kelly purchased stickers of Easter chicks to promote her icon and had great results.

Developing my personal icon took several years. It's still being perfected as will your own personal icon. Don't worry if the idea doesn't just enter your mind right now. But if something does come to you right away, start playing with it.

Interests and Hobbies

Do you have a hobby that helps people remember you? Maybe you have a passion for knitting. Can this be related to your business (key point here—your icon has got to relate back to your company and/or product)? You could carry a sample of your knitting to your shows and let people know you love to knit people together with your product and opportunity.

Personal Icons Carry On

Apply your personal icon to everything you do. When you get a letter from me, what color of envelopes and stationery do you think I use? Yellow! Some people say they know it's from me even if the envelope is turned so they only see the back. I'm fortunate that many of my direct sales friends who represent stamp companies have lemon stamps for me to use. Your personal icon is your theme and it will become your brand.

Business Cards

One way to follow through on your personal icon is with your business card. Personally, my business card is a real package of lemonade. Everyone keeps it—exactly what I want them to do!

Let me give you some examples from others. My friend Teresa is a successful consultant with Petra Fashions®. When I first met her, I was excited that she gave me $20 cash! Wasn't that a nice of her? Upon closer examination, I saw it was just part of a small, fake twenty dollar bill. But when I opened it up, Teresa's name and phone number were there. That's a card I'll never throw out! I call her Twenty Dollar Teresa.

Another friend with Petra Fashions is Shirley. She also uses pretend money as her business card. At the end of a class she handed me what I thought was a silver dollar. Instead, it was a mock coin with her contact information on it—a real *TWIST* on a business card! Even though her coin is not negotiable, I'd never throw it away! I remember her as "Silver Shirley."

One of my non-direct sales clients is a massage therapist. On her business card is her slogan, "Massage is a real life saver for reducing daily stress." When she hands out a business card, she gives the recipient a wrapped Life Saver® candy. And she never lacks for appointments…

How Personal Icons Attract more Hostesses

You probably have a magnet of some sort on your refrigerator right now. When you placed the magnet on your fridge, what happened as the magnet got near the fridge? It attached itself to the fridge, didn't it! Is that because the fridge is made out of the same materials as the magnet? Of course not...they have different properties. So you see, when you're different—not the same old stuff—more hostesses will be attracted to you! Be a human magnet because you're different and you manifest that difference and place yourself in peoples' minds with your personal icon.

When you're different—not the same old stuff—more hostesses will be attracted to you!

Segment Five

Time is More Money…and More Bookings

One of the most frequent reasons we hear "no" when inviting people to book classes and shows is "I don't have time." Next time you hear that sentence, don't attempt to overcome the objection, rather, add two extra words in your own mind: *to waste*. Because what people are really saying is "I don't have time *to waste*." Many people want to buy your product and listen to your presentation and even host a party with you. What none of us wants to do is waste time. In reality, we can all make time for what's important…we just want that time to be of value to us.

As demonstrators, we can be in control of time more than what we are so that we don't waste anyone's time—including our own. For more than 15 years, I held six-to-eight classes every week. Since then, I attend as many home demonstrations as possible. Partly so I can do research in preparing company presentations and mostly because I love to attend. As a guest, I've felt my time being wasted many times by the demonstrator—before, during and after the presentation. If time is one of our constraints on booking more shows, let's do the *TWIST* and discover how we can make time more valuable to guests, hostesses, consultants and everyone's families. This means making the most of everyone's time before, during, and after a presentation.

Before the Party Preparation

Before the presentation, be prepared. This way, when you get to the hostess' home, you're not making last minute preparations such as putting catalogs into binders, putting stickers on order forms, etc. Always do this: Pretend that you'll be stuck in traffic so when you walk into the hostess home, everyone is there waiting for you (I know this sounds like a nightmare; keep reading….). Would you be able to walk right in and begin talking and teaching by simply pulling your products out of your case/bag/box/basket? This is an illustration just to show that all extra tasks should be done ahead of time at your home.

I realize some of you do cooking, stamping, scrapping, making up faces, and other "hands on" demonstrations (my favorite kind!). Just have all the materials prepared so you can walk in and begin if need be.

Many times I had to depend on the hostess to be prepared with

40

supplies. Calling her the night before doesn't insure she'd be ready, only that she'd know my expectations. I also asked her to do all the steps she could. So, if I sold knives and needed to demonstrate how well they chop a green pepper, I would ask the hostess to have the green pepper all washed and sitting on the counter top. I would explain that the more we're both prepared, the less time we'll take at the party. This strategy also eliminated my having to get to her house too early (remember – your time is valuable too!).

Now, you're probably waiting for me to tell you how early to get to a hostess' home. Every situation is unique, but my advice is to be there with enough time to be ready to meet and greet guests 15 to 20 minutes before the class starts. If people aren't arriving that soon, use this time to collect any orders the hostess already has. Once this is completed, offer the hostess assistance while she prepares snacks and other tasks. I've even held a hostess' baby while she went to get dressed.

The number one rule for hostesses is: Hostesses Rule. You are a guest in her home.

On-Time without Offending

Here's a scenario you've probably experienced: It's 7:00 p.m.— you know the traditional time to start a home party—and you're all ready to get on with the show. You turn to your hostess and say, "It's 7:00, time to get started." What do most hostesses say?

The usual response is "I've got a few more people that are coming; can we wait a while?" Now, I believe that the number one rule for hostesses is: Hostesses Rule. You are a guest in her home.

You should never say, "No way! We agreed to start at 7:00! I'm paying for a baby sitter, and besides, tonight is my favorite TV show at 9:30. We've got to get started so I can get home—we're starting on time and we'll end on time!"

I'm hoping this response is a real exaggeration and that no one would ever treat a hostess that way! If I were a hostess and a demonstrator said that to me, I'd invite her to leave immediately— that way she wouldn't have to worry about her childcare or her TV show; just running out of business. This example might be a bit extreme, but I've personally heard demonstrators say some cutting remarks to hostesses. Any statement that would not make a hostess feel special should not be spoken. And remember that her guests can hear most conversations, so be especially careful about what you say—and convey.

On the other hand, what about the guests that are already there?

They might have left work early to get to the class on time. Maybe they even did a drive-through dinner for their family so they could get to your demonstration on time. You need to respect them and their punctuality. But what about this dilemma—waiting for others? And the "others" are often the mother and sisters of the hostess. What do you do? Remember, the purpose of this book—and your business—is to attract more hostesses. Here is one of the best ways— let's do the Lemon Aid *TWIST*.

For this illustration, my hostess is Beth. And when she says, "Please wait, I have a few more people coming," I enthusiastically reply, "That's great; the more the merrier! While we're waiting, do you mind if I share a few *value-added* ideas with the people who are here?" Well, who could say "no" to an offer like that? Let me explain *value-added* ideas.

First, you can call these *extra tips* a fun name relative to your company. At our Learning Adventures, I say "an extra squeeze." If you sell make up, you might call them "Beauty Bonuses." If you're a consultant for a company who sells bowls of any kind, you could call it "Bonus Bowl Time." The idea is to position this part of your presentation as something special, something extra. You're rewarding the ladies who are on time without penalizing those who might be caught in traffic, taking kids to a sitter (that's worth waiting for!), or who are simply late. I only ask the hostess' permission so that all the guests hear; now they feel like they're really getting their time's worth!

This segment of the demonstration takes about ten minutes; go with the flow—it could be less or longer, but not much on either side. And, just what are you going to share with them? First let me tell you what not to share. Don't teach them anything that is essential for the entire group to hear. This is basic information that anyone who attends a class needs to be taught. You'll have to make that decision according to your company. I always liked sharing an extra quick and simple recipe. Depending on your product line you could do tips on accessories, decorating, quick stamping, tying scarves, etc. Some of my best ideas for this segment came from reading women's magazines and *twisting* the ideas to my product.

I also like highlighting sets of products during this *value-added* time. These sets do not have to be something pre-packaged from your company. Nor do they have to be sets with a special price—simply add the cost of each item and that's the *set price*. When you teach a concept and then give a package price, it's easier for people to order. Most people purchase what you demonstrate first or what you demonstrate last. And some of these guests might only get to stay for a half an hour, so what they see first is important to them.

What are most guests thinking about this service? Most are enthralled with your fun, creative tips (be sure they are fun and creative) and believe you are so wonderful because you're essentially starting on time. This gives them another reason to "hire" you to come to their home: you're adding value to—not taking from—their precious time

During this *value-added* segment, your hostess is busy answering the door, taking coats, getting drinks for her friends, etc. So don't expect her to be sitting down and listening; she's being a hostess (not just in the party plan sense) by taking care of her guests. If you can help to entertain her friends and teach new ideas at the same time, everyone wins. And, more people in this group tend to book with you because you honored their time by starting on time—even though you really haven't started yet!

Value-added ideas give them another reason to "hire" you to come to their home: you're adding value to—not taking from—their precious time.

What about the people who are still coming in? Because you have center stage, you'll be meeting and greeting with a *TWIST*. As they walk in, they begin apologizing and explaining their tardiness. You simply smile and say: "Oh, we haven't started the party yet; we're just sharing some bonus tips. "Come on in!" These ladies feel welcome for attending, rather than embarrassed for coming late. The adage "Better late than never" certainly applies in this case. As these late-comers arrive, they know they've missed something important and curiously ask: "What did I miss? If you're using the order forms prepared with their names, (See *Paper Potential*) or have binders or other literature and handouts that you've been giving to people as you meet and greet them, give these to your hostess so she can distribute them as the guests arrive.

As you give these *value-added* tips, people will begin telling their friends: "You've got to go to her shows early because she starts on time with these great ideas." As these people book from your demonstrations, more will show up on time because they want to get the *value-added* ideas. You don't have to give anything away except your expertise—something that can't be bought!

After I've shared the Value Added tips, I've essentially begun the demonstration without really beginning. When I'm finished, and the hostess is in the room, I turn to her and ask: "Can we get started now?" The guests are already involved, the momentum has begun, and I don't believe a hostess ever said she wanted to wait any longer. Are all the people she was expecting there? Probably not. Some never do arrive! So, it's time to get on with the show and spotlight the hostess.

At this point, you can proceed to the segment on *Allow her to Introduce You.* Or, keep reading more ways about *Time is More Money and More Bookings*. The choice is yours!

How Long Should a Home Party Last?

You might have thought this segment is only about starting on time. But that's only part of the time issue. The next timely situation to consider is how long the home party should last. Notice I didn't say, how long should your demonstration be. Note that the length of your demonstration will largely determine the length of the party.

First, let's discuss your demonstration. The average sitcom on TV is 30 minutes. But of those 30 minutes, about eight are taken up in commercials. The commercials are timed to give the average mind a break approximately every eight minutes—the attention span of most adults. So, if your presentation is a full hour without any activity breaks (See the segments on *Take Part of the Action* and *Featured Attractions*), you're going to have a lot of people looking at their watches, getting anxious, and feeling like their time is being wasted. These are the people that tell you "I don't have time [to waste]" when you invite them to be a hostess.

I've found that short, sweet, and on-time demonstrations are appealing to most guests. What consultants want to show and tell the audience is really important to *consultants*, but is this the most important information for the guests? I've cut out many parts of my demonstrations when we were not able to start on time (even with the *value-added* tips, sometimes the start can be delayed), had unexpected interruptions, or I felt the guests had "had enough." Be in tune with your audience—that's your best indicator. Some of the very best home demonstrations I've attended as a guest were less than 30 minutes long—that again was the actual demonstration part.

A couple comments that you'll want to strive for is to hear people say, "Keep talking...these ideas are so good!" Or, "This demo was the best I've seen; I can't believe it's time to go home!" In other words, you'll want to have quenched their thirst for what they came for…and made them thirsty again for more information! As you do this, the comments you hear will be *TWISTED* to the greatest business compliments you'll ever receive when several people say, "I enjoyed myself so much, I'm booking a class with you." Notice this is a two-part compliment—the first part is words and the second part is action! This compliment comes about when they feel the time they spent was valuable.

When Should the Party End?

What is the longest part of a home presentation: the demonstration or the ordering? In almost all circumstances it's the *ordering*. My husband is a good sport when he goes shopping with me. He's also very patient. I'll go to a store to purchase something specific, but on the way through, my eye catches sight of all kinds of other things I might just need. And as a woman, I'm like a lot of your guests: I have a hard time making up my mind! When a guest has a tantalizing catalog in front of her and she just witnessed a fabulous presentation, she is confused. Should she buy or not? Maybe she should just take the catalog home with her (how many times do we hear that?). Will her husband mind? Does she have the money in her budget? Should she use one payment plan or all three (cash, check, credit cards). So many decisions and so little time! And she'll use all the time you give her.

The greatest business compliment you'll ever receive is when several people say: "I enjoyed myself so much, I'm booking a class with you."

Have you ever been to a store just before closing? On the loud speaker, you hear something like, "Thank you for shopping at your local grocery store. Our store will be closing in ten minutes. Please have your purchases ready and come to the check out." If they didn't announce this, people would continue shopping for hours!

The way to shorten the long, drawn out ordering process is to give the guests a deadline as you finish your presentation:

> "Ladies, I hope you've enjoyed the presentation tonight as much as I have; you're such a fun group. I'll be happy to service you and help you with your questions and orders until 8:30. Then I promised Beth I'd be on my way so she can get her babies in bed."

Now, what have I just given my guests: a deadline! Okay, I can hear you asking: "What if she doesn't have kids to put to bed?" I'd say: "I promised Beth I'd be on my way by 8:30 because I know she gets up early for work." In other words adapt this to your hostess' situation. At some parties with huge attendance, I might actually be there 15 or 20 minutes longer than I "promised." That's because I'm helping a lot of people; I'm not sitting down twiddling my thumbs while people are eating and then ordering.

Here's a tip to speed up the "accounting process." Purchase inexpensive calculators. Place them around the room along with tax charts. Encourage guests to add up their orders and add the tax. Of course, if someone is unsure of how to figure her order, you'll give her assistance. Invite them to meet with you to "scan" the order form. You quickly check to see they've indicated color, size, etc. Take particular notice of the "future boxes" that she checks if she wants to buy, book, or sell in the future. (See *Paper Potential* for ways to focus on these important boxes.) If you spend all your night adding up orders and playing accountant, you'll miss scheduling opportunities. When you get home and see someone has made a mistake, simply give her a call. This really speeds up the ordering process and allows you time to do what benefits the most people: book and recruit!

By speeding up the ordering process, you can finish your portion of the party. There is no harm in packing up your display while people are still thumbing through the catalogs—face it; some people are not going to order even if you're in their faces. Again, I give a "deadline" by stating:

> "I'll be picking up my display in the next five minutes. Feel free to come up and look closer at any of the items during that time."

Am I giving you the deadline ideas so you can get home, release your sitter, and watch the 9:30 program? No...I'm giving you this suggestion so that you'll book more shows. You are conveying to your hostess and her guests that their time is valuable. You've done what you've promised: given a great demonstration, serviced the people, and scheduled more business.

After I put my products away, I pull the hostess aside from her guests—this is when they are chatting and eating—and explain the sales and bookings she has so far. Now, she knows where she stands with regard to her hostess gifts. Perhaps your company provides a list you can leave her so she knows if she needs to collect payment from anyone. I remind her of another deadline: when I need to have all the orders and payments. I then explain: "You only need _____ sales and _____ bookings to get the gifts you want." Or, Congratulations! You made your goal!" I normally don't wait for her to tell me what gifts she wants because she's visiting and wants some time to decide. I make an appointment to call her for that information.

After this, I can leave. If her guests choose to stay, that's up to them and the hostess. But you are not holding up their departure in any way. The guests see that you're not going to be camping at the hostess' house all night. And if her husband has left with the children for the evening, it's nice to be finished or be on the way to being finished when he returns, assuming he's not out just for an hour.

Many times, my hostess invited me to stay for dessert. I always teased and said "Thanks so much; everything looks yummy! But I have to restrain myself because if I ate at every class…I'd be pretty big!" And, she'd laugh, and understand.

Be Brief *(say what the guests need to know in a short time)*. Be Bright *(have fun, be happy, entertain and educate)*. Be Gone *(leave on time)*.

As with everything in this business, you go with the flow. If you feel like you want to get to know some of the people better, and it's not late, being social might be better than leaving. Also, know their culture. Some hostesses would be offended if I didn't have a bite to eat with them and their friends. Thank heaven our industry is never boring; every day we go to work, we have a different audience. The key is to do what you feel is the best in that situation. While we don't ever want to waste anyone's time, we also don't want to offend a hostess and her guests.

To summarize, I remember something I was taught in the beginning of my direct sales career with regard to how long a home party should last from beginning to end: Be *Brief* (say what the guests need to know in a short time). Be *Bright* (have fun, be happy, entertain and educate). Be *Gone* (leave on time).

Extra Lemon Squeeze with a timely *TWIST:*

Because you're reading a book, you can choose the time and place you do this. So, rather than give a real illustration of a *Value - Added Idea* at the beginning of this segment, when you might not know what I'm talking about, I'm putting this idea at the end. One, you'll feel what getting something extra feels like, and two, this idea will give you more time for more bookings in your book because you are going to be very busy as you begin implementing these tips. So, here's an *Extra Lemon Squeeze* for you:

Years ago our family moved from the Detroit, Michigan Metropolitan area, where I had built a substantial business in three years, to the suburbs of Salt Lake City, Utah. This was not the first time I had moved my business; however, it was the most difficult. I was getting rather discouraged because I was accustomed to higher party sales; my average in my new area was less than half of what I was used to.

I finally did something many of us neglect to do: I consulted with my sales leader, Valerie. She had grown a very successful business in the area, so I knew she must know the "secret." She suggested I hold more than one demonstration a day, and taught me a business-changing concept of holding two demonstrations a night! She explained that at that time I might have to work twice as hard to get the results I was used to.

I had previously held daytime demonstrations, but people did not normally request them. But to hold two parties in one evening? I wondered how I could do that. How could I get from one to another? How could I even schedule that many? Would people be open to starting parties at 6:00 and 8:00 p.m. as Valerie suggested? Isn't there some kind of *law* that says all home parties begin at 7:00 p.m.? Valerie shared her experiences and tips with me, and with that information and some new *TWISTS* of my own, I reluctantly decided to give the idea a try. If this didn't work (actually the more accurate statement is "if I didn't work this idea"), I knew I'd be leaving the business.

The first thing I did was to decide myself when I wanted to hold daytime events. For me, those days were Wednesday and Thursday. I put in two time slots for that—10:00 a.m. and 1:00 p.m. This way, my boys would be off to school and I'd be home before they returned. Then I decided which evenings I'd want to hold two shows. I simply chose the evenings that I was already working: Tuesday, Wednesday, and Thursday. Please keep in mind that I share my time schedule only as a teaching aid; you can choose the days and times best for you and your family. I was also open to other evenings and Saturdays if my customers requested and I didn't have previous commitments with my family or church; however, I pretty much used this schedule week after week.

Next, I took a green highlighter and on my calendar, I put green lines on those time slots. (I like green because it reminds me of growth; by coincidence, green is also the color of American dollars!). On these lines, I wrote in the times: 10:00 a.m., 1:00, 6:00 and 8:00 p.m. As I began booking these classes, my first question to a new hostess was "Do you prefer a day time or evening party?" Interestingly, some people had no idea that we could lawfully hold parties during the day! And, a lot of people are home during the day. Elderly people who don't like driving after dark loved this idea. Young moms appreciated getting together with other moms and their kids.

For those who wanted an evening event, my next question was, "Which is the best time for you 6:00 or 8:00?" This is when I had some surprised people who asked: "What about 7:00?" My reply was: "Because I am in such demand for demonstrations, I've had to open up two time slots each evening. And, this way, you can be assured that having a class with me is not going to take all night." Then I asked if they and their friends worked at jobs that required them to get up really early. If so, the 6:00 p.m. would be best for them. If, on the other hand, they and their friends didn't get home from work until after 6 or 6:30, then 8:00 would work best for them. People readily agreed.

We've been discussing how people explain their reason for not booking as: "I don't have time [to waste]." As I began offering different time slots, I discovered what some people meant was: "I don't have time during the time slots when you hold parties." I found that these non-traditional party hours became a great service and a way to reach people who had non-traditional work hours, such as hospital staff members. Further, when someone said: "My friends go to PTA on Wednesday." I'd ask: "What time is the meeting?" When we figured out that a lot of meetings started at 6:30 or 7:00 and ended at 7:30 or 8:00, my hostesses felt like an 8:00 start time would work. This way, people weren't leaving their houses every night for something different. Instead, they just had one busy night where they accomplished much.

Non-traditional party hours become a great service and a way to reach people who have non-traditional work hours.

During my hostess planning sessions, I encouraged the 6:00 hostess to be sure her friends were on time (of course this rarely happened, so we did the *value-added* tips), and that I'd be available for them until 7:30—about the time they were starting to have their refreshments (remember that earlier in this segment I taught you about giving a deadline).

My 8:00 hostess was a little different. I suggested she still invite people for 7:30 and that she begin serving refreshments as the people arrive (now, if you are a consultant for a cooking or kitchen company where you prepare the food, she can begin serving the beverages.) And, this is important, I asked her to announce to her guests that I'd be arriving at 8:00—on time to begin the presentation. Only once did I have a guest, who was also a former consultant with my company—you know, the one who seems to know everything—who said: "You're late!" I nicely explained the schedule to her.

At my 6:00 class, after my demonstration, I did announce: "I'll be here to service you until 7:30 and then I'll be on my way to my next party." Well, people were flabbergasted! They wondered how I could "get" more than one party in a night! As they scheduled new parties with me; however, they would brag to their friends about having a consultant who is so good she "holds two parties a night."

Once in a while I would have a 6:00 party and not have one dated for 8:00. In that case, I did the same thing only I got home earlier that night. I simply announced, "I'll be here to service you until 7:30 and then I'll be on my way to my next appointment." This helps in your schedule as well. Perhaps you have a church meeting every Wednesday night at 8:00 and thought you couldn't work that night; guess what? Now you can!!

On to the 8:00 party. Before we go further, I hope you realize that logistically your two shows must be close together. I'll give you a hint in a few minutes how this will help you book more. I wanted my driving distance to be not more than ten minutes apart (once in a while, I might not leave the 6:00 class till 7:40, so I had to be close). As I arrived at my next hostess' home, I did not worry about setting up a display. I simply walked in and announced: "Let the fun begin." And I started the demonstration as I began taking my products out of my carrier.

You might be thinking: "Wait a minute, what about being there ahead of time, *meeting and greeting, value-added ideas*, etc." You should know one of my favorite sayings is: "Every situation is situational." I learned this from my Organizational Behavior college professor, and it's so true. In other words, those *Meet and Greet* concepts might not be practical in this case. You are the one who has to decide. You'll also see that in the scenario of two-parties-a-night, you'll use other ideas I've taught and that you'll be reading as you go along—like *Taking Part of the Action*. Those ideas work great in these cases.

The people at the 8:00 party have already eaten and visited. They're usually ready to listen. And at the end of your presentation, they are ready to go home, so they don't linger much longer and you're on your way home at about the same time as if your event had begun at 7:00 or 7:30. The difference is, you left home a little earlier and you made twice as much progress in your business.

As my business expanded geographically and I was driving over an hour to a hostess' home, I'd go through my records to see who I knew it the area. After all, if I'm driving a distance, why not accomplish twice as much? I'd call people in that city: "Janey, Good News!! I'm doing a class in your area on Wednesday the 26th at 6:00; I have an 8:00 opening where I could fit in a party for you." I was always amazed, and very pleased, at the "yeses." People like to do business with successful people. I exuded success because of my schedule. Literally, I had people come into a class and right away ask to be on my calendar because they knew how busy and successful I was. Then they'd say to the other people: "If you want to have a class with her, you better let her know now."

Now, I know some of you are arguing with me in your minds, saying: "But I sell clothing that needs to be tried on; we can't do that all in two hours." Or: "I do cooking demonstrations, I need more time that what you're suggesting." I, too, did a lot of cooking classes. Most of my parties had this format. Remember, you're in control of how much time you take and the information you give out. I believe you can do whatever you want to. And of course, I also teach you the *TWIST*. Perhaps you can offer demonstrations at 5:00 and 8:00. You choose. I just found the people appreciated I was flexible for their schedule.

I can't begin to tell you how positively this idea affects your recruiting. I could honestly say to prospects: "I have so much business; our company really needs more consultants!"

I did have a couple nay sayers telling me that I shouldn't be holding "so many parties" (I detected just a hint of jealousy). Then I'd ask that person how many hours a week she was away from home for her job. Notice I didn't ask how many hours she worked; I wanted to know door-to-door time: when she left her home to when she returned. The answer was usually over 50 hours a week. Even holding eight parties a week at four hours a party (way more than I'd ever take), that's less than 35 hours from home! It's amazing.

I'm also not suggesting you do this every night and day of every week. However, it's a great idea if you're limited on the evenings you can work. I know many consultants who have full-time jobs along with their direct sales business and others who, because of family circumstances, can only devote one or two evenings a week to their businesses. This concept is an ideal way to multiply all aspects of your business.

And, I can't begin to tell you how positively this idea affects your recruiting. I could honestly say to prospects: "I have so much business; our company really needs more consultants!" Because I was holding more classes, I also had the opportunity to meet more prospects and I had more shows to take new people with me for training.

This brings me to my last point. You can really become an expert at holding multiple parties in a day if you have an assistant. My choice was new people who were learning about the business. Sometimes I had a new consultant who could only attend the 8:00 class. That was fine. She was able to learn as she assisted me. If my class had been at 7:00, sometimes her work schedule didn't allow her to attend that early.

I can't stress the benefits of being more flexible to add more time slots to your book enough. You've just got to try it to believe it! Soon, people will be asking if you have time to do a demonstration for them!

Segment Six

Allow Her to Introduce You

As you wind up your value-added ideas (if you need to use them), and the guests are settling in, it's time to get on with the show…and the spotlight is first on your hostess.

Before I explain this next segment on attracting more hostesses at presentations, let's go back to the time when you're planning the class with your hostess. Again, Beth is my hostess, and I ask:

> "Beth, would you mind reading a short introduction that I've prepared at the beginning of your class so that your friends will know a little about me before I begin?"

Now, I've never had a hostess tell me *no*.

Keep the planning conversation flowing:

> "So that I can have the Introduction prepared, please tell me what made you decide to have a show with me."

The words are coming from someone they know—and trust. This is a third-person testimonial, and is one of the most powerful forms of promotion. It's "word of mouth" with a TWIST because the whole group is listening.

Let her explain (this response gives you great insight into why people book—or don't book—with you!). You might need to *prod* her just a bit: Did she like the "make and take" from the last class, is she wanting to show off her new home, is there a special hostess incentive that she wants, etc. You'll see in a few minutes why I need this.

Let's go back to the beginning of her class. As you finish the "value added" tips, or if you started right on time, give the hostess a nod and prompt her that she can now read your introduction. By the way, I mail or e-mail this to her in advance so she can look it over. I also bring a hard copy with me in case she forgot or misplaced hers. Here's an example of what you might have prepared for her:

> "Hi Friends!! It's great that you could all be here tonight at my _____ (name of company) demonstration. You know, the best part of the show/class/workshop/party, is_____ (your name), my _____ consultant. I met her at _____ (name of hostess she booked from, or grocery store, soccer team, elevator, etc.) and

decided to have this event because _____
(this is where you fill in the reason she gave you as to why
she booked with you). _____
(your name) has been with _____
(your company) for _____(years/months).

"She has been recognized for _____
(list one of your best accomplishments—if you're brand
new, announce that you're the number one consultant on
_____ your Street/Drive/Lane—
because you're probably the one only on your street—and
you're new—and that's the truth!).

"Now, let's welcome _____
(your name).

Write in the words, "Clap for Consultant." As she claps, her
friends do too, and you're warming up to them.

Does this sound a little silly to you? I hope so. It's also very
different—have you ever been to a home party and the hostess
introduced the consultant? Most haven't—unless the consultant is
a Lemon Aid Learner!

How do most consultants begin their parties? This is what I did for
years: "Hi, my name is Christie [sounds like I'm giving a speech
for high school student body elections!], I've been with Northrup
Party Plan for a long time, I love what I do, you should join me
because I set my own hours and make as much money as I want
to." Boring. Boring. Boring! And, everybody starts the same way!

So, how does this simple step attract more hostesses at your
shows? Because even though their friend is reading what you've
written (and the hostess often embellishes your script with more
accolades), the words are coming from someone they know—and
trust. This is a third-person testimonial, and is one of the most
powerful forms of promotion. It's "word of mouth" with a *TWIST*
because the whole group is listening. Which makes you want to do
the very best presentation ever because the words keep going
through many mouths!

Additionally, when the hostess tells "why" she booked with you,
she often mentions what hostess gift she is working for; she is the
one who is non-verbally inviting her friends to buy and book from
you to help her. You don't have to *TWIST* anyone's arms or minds
with words like, "If any of you are real friends of Beth's, you'll get
out your credit cards and calendars and buy and book—that's the

name of the game." Now, that's pushy!! In fact, you'll be pushing people away!

Here's another reason why I love the hostess to introduce the consultant: RECRUITING! After the introduction, depending on the hostess and the group (remember go with the flow how you feel), I sometimes tease by saying:

> "Beth! That was a great introduction! You've now passed the _____ (company name) audition and can join me as a consultant."

Or, you might feel the following is a better approach: As you're tallying up the sales and have some one-on-one time with the hostess, mention:

> "Beth, you did such a great job reading my introduction. You'd be a natural consultant!"

> Let her respond.

Another scenario might be that you talked with Beth prior to her class, and she indicated that she'd love to be a consultant like you, but just has a huge fear of getting up and speaking in front of people. This is a real fear for many...a fear they've been able to overcome by doing group demonstrations. After the party, you're having an individual conversation with her and say:

> "Beth, I think I have you confused with someone else. Before your class when I shared the information about joining my team, you said you had a huge fear of speaking in front of people. Yet, you did such an excellent job on the introduction; I must have you confused with someone else."

Then she tells you that you're not confused; she really has a great fear and that reading your introduction was simple because you gave her the words to say and she spoke them to her family and friends. You can explain that when she becomes a consultant, her first presentations will be with people she knows like her family and friends—and you'll even give her the words to say.

This simple conversation can be a real "aha" moment for her if she, indeed, has this fear and it's not just an excuse. By using the *Allow her to Introduce You* concept, not only will you have more hostesses attracted to you, but also more new recruits!

By using the **Allow her to Introduce You** *concept, not only will you have more hostesses attracted to you, but also more new recruits!*

Segment Seven

Thank You, Two

I'm sure one of the rituals you always perform at a demonstration is to thank your hostess in front of her guests so she really feels special and appreciated. You want everyone to be envious of the hostess and think, or say: "I want all the attention, accolades, and gifts that's she's getting." So, after she has read my introduction, and I *come on down*, I have the hostess stand by me so I can present her with some extra surprises—remember, anything you give should be very valuable, yet inexpensive! The Booster (1-800-5JENNYB) has some excellent suggestions.

As the hostess sits down, I make another announcement:

> "There's another person here tonight who I want to thank. In fact, if it weren't for her, none of us would be here. Please give a round of thanks to Amy—the person Beth booked her party from. Amy, come on down!"

If you refer back to the *Top 40* in the *Pre-Presentation* Segment, you'll remember the first person I encourage my new hostesses to invite is the person she booked her party from. My "Thank You, Two" segment is the reason I want that previous hostess in attendance.

Before the party, I've chosen one of my products that looks like it could be a microphone (yes, you read that right—a microphone). Think of a product you sell that might fit the bill—I mean mic. I'd choose something like a belt, rolled up napkin, wire whisk, salt shaker, taper candle etc. Why a microphone? Because you'll be like Barbara Walters and interview this previous hostess—with her permission, of course!

Let's go back to the workshop: Remember, tonight's hostess is Amy. I just honored her and now I've recognized the previous hostess, who is now standing next to me. I proceed:

> "Beth, you are the person we can all thank for our being here tonight. Do you mind if I ask you a few questions about being one of my hostesses?"

She says, "yes."

Before interviewing her, I ask: "Do you mind if I use my handy dandy microphone?"

At this time, you use the designated product. People in the audience begin to laugh. And when they laugh...they listen! And, now I have a product literally in someone's face without being offensive. Your guests get a real kick out of this, and your previous hostess will be at ease.

The first question is always: "Did you enjoy being a hostess?" Again, the answer will be "yes." Rather than share a dialog at this point of the book, I'm going to list other questions you can ask her. Before you get to this present demonstration, review the statistics from your previous class so you can help answer the questions if needed. I can read your mind as you're reading this book...I'll cover some of your "what ifs" after the questions.

Interview the previous hostess by asking her two or three questions about her hostess experience.

- How many people were at your class?
- What kind of a class did we do? (See the segment on *Featured Attractions*)
- Do you remember how much you had in sales?
- Did you receive any gifts?
- What are some of the gifts?
- Do you know the dollar value of the gifts?
- How many of your friends scheduled their own demonstration?
- Would you recommend being a hostess with me to anyone else?

Now, regardless of which questions you choose to ask (and do feel free to make up your own rather than the ones I listed) you always end with the following question:

"Beth, thanks for sharing your experience. Are you looking forward to being a hostess again?"

Now, I haven't had anyone say "no" to this question in front of the group. This is not to imply that they said yes and always held another. But, this is a key question and gets the previous hostess thinking about rebooking.

Here are answers to the questions going through your mind right now. If the previous hostess is not in attendance, obviously you won't have this opportunity to use this concept. Nor will you use this idea if you booked the class away from a party; like at the school fundraiser where there was no hostess.

And, what if the previous presentation wasn't much to brag about?

I believe there is always something good and unique from every demonstration. Focus on what was positive. Perhaps her show was the night of the biggest snowstorm of the season. You can congratulate her for having three people who braved the storm. In all cases, keep it very positive. It accentuates the positive for her, too. If she felt like she had let you down because her show was not up to your normal standards of sales and attendance, you're focusing on what you appreciated from her, and expressing that appreciation in front of a group. Obviously, one of the most positive aspects of her party was that you are now in front of a new group of people—all thanks to her.

At this point, I also present her with another gift. This is very valuable yet very inexpensive—what other kinds would I give? At every class, I take a picture of the hostess and her friends. You can also have someone take a picture of you with the hostess and/or the guests. I use disposable cameras for this; digitals are very nice, too. I just don't want to be concerned about losing something like an expensive digital camera. And, using a disposable will motivate you to hold a regular schedule of shows so that you can get the film developed in a timely manner.

If you're creative, represent a stamp or scrapbook company, or know demonstrators in these businesses, you can create a scrapbook page for the hostess, or make a very simple frame. Of course you can also buy frames from some of our friends in other direct sales companies. Whichever way you choose, give her this memorable souvenir of her party.

Always get double prints and create a *Business Brag Book* of your hostesses to take to your shows. You can use some of the testimonials from the interviews in the album. This is another way to attract more hostesses because they'll be in your special book! For more suggestions about this idea, refer to page 87 of the *Lemon Aid Deed Alphabet* as well as the Segment 12, *The Party's Over*.

Why does this work?

Let's discuss why using Thank You, Two would add more bookings to your calendar. Have you ever demonstrated hostess gifts or explained the hostess program at your presentation just to see the looks of "I could never qualify for those kinds of gifts" on the faces of the guests?

Well, after you interview a hostess who has actually qualified for these gifts, and you're not the only one talking about the hostess benefits (remember the third person testimonial in the previous segment on *Allow Her to Introduce You*), other people will take action. Additionally, maybe the previous hostess only had three people in attendance. The guests sitting at your show tonight who really want to say "yes" but don't think they know enough people will be thinking: "Wow, if she went to a party with only three people, maybe she'll come to mine. I know at least five people will definitely come."

The bottom line is they are hearing the experiences of other people and thus feel a lot less intimidated. Because you'll become so confident (not to be confused with cocky), some people really will feel like they're not good enough to be your hostess. But, with this method, you'll help everyone feel at ease. Of course, you don't want to advertise that you do mediocre shows. However, many times this person or this party might not be the *clinker* (the one that puts "cha-ching cash" in your bank account), but they can always be a Lemon Aid Linker—linking you to someone else who will be the clinker!

Both hostesses feel and believe: "Wow, she made me feel special." The biggest craving any of us have as a human is to be appreciated. And with this concept, you're showing appreciation.

This idea also encourages past hostesses to attend the classes of those people who booked from them. This is a nice feeling for everyone. In this case, Beth has seen me recognize the previous hostess so she is eager to attend Amy's party. And, Amy will also be eager to attend the bookings from her shows, so she and Beth both encourage others to be future hostesses. Both hostesses feel and believe: "Wow, she made me feel special." Do you know the biggest craving any of us have as a human is to be appreciated? That's our biggest craving. And with this concept, you're showing appreciation.

Now, what if Amy has three bookings, should you do this at all of the ones she attends? Of course. You might want to change the questions a bit and also give her different souvenirs.

More *TWISTS*

Another *TWIST* is to recognize all of your previous hostesses at each party. You can do this in addition, or instead of, highlighting only the previous hostess. You can make a candy bouquet (a bunch of candy bars or other candy tied together—this is definitely inexpensive—but very valuable) and have each previous hostess pick one. I use the candy bar wrappers from The Booster.

Remember, these people are not just previous hostesses with your company, but previous hostesses *with you*. If you're at a show and only three people are not part of this exclusive group, the others will book so they can be in the group as well. Additionally, when one of your previous hostesses is invited to one of your presentations, she'll be even more excited to attend when she knows she'll get extra attention as one of your hostesses.

If your company has special recognition and rewards for people who host multiple demonstrations in a calendar year, or who have been a hostess within the past 12 months, remind this group of those benefits and invite everyone else to join their elite club of previous—and future—hostesses.

You can do another *TWIST*. Each month or quarter recognize the hostess who has the most previous hostesses at her class. If you're complaining, "I've only held 16 shows in my whole career, this just wouldn't work," quit whining and start booking!

In all, you'll be recognizing and rewarding repeat and referred business—a simple and effective way of adding dozens and dozens more bookings to your calendar.

Segment Eight

Featured Attractions

It's Saturday night and you're going to the movies! You walk up to the box office at the mega cinema (you know those with thirty-plus screens), hand the attendant a ten dollar bill and ask for a ticket. The first question you'll be asked is, "Which movie do you want to see?" Have you ever said, "I don't care; just give me a ticket for any one of them." Of course not. You wouldn't waste your money and time seeing something you have no interest in.

Word-of-mouth advertising cannot be purchased in any medium—it's priceless and oh so valuable.

Just why do people flock to the big screens every week? The movie entertainment industry is a multi-billion dollar industry, and we all watch movies for one of the following reasons:

1. We want to be *entertained and have a night out*. Maybe this is time with our kids, spouse, or friends. We just want to kick back and watch.
2. The *subject matter*—whether it's science fiction, romance, or comedy—is of interest to us.
3. The *lead actress or actor* is one of our favorites. I personally love movies with Tom Hanks or Denzel Washington. If we don't like an actor/actress, we sometimes avoid those movies even if we hear great things about them.
4. *Previews or trailers* entice us to go to a movie. We might have seen the preview when we were at the last movie. Maybe it was a trailer on television. Whichever way, we were curious and intrigued—enough to part with some cash and time.
5. Probably the reason most of us go is because *someone else told us* about this movie that we just cannot miss. Of all the reasons, this is the most powerful way Hollywood sells seats. You've probably gone to a movie you never saw advertised only because someone else told someone who told someone who told you. And you went and *told others* about it! This is simply word-of-mouth advertising. This kind of exposure cannot be purchased in any medium—it's priceless and oh so valuable.

Are you wondering what going to the movies has to do with booking more of your own company shows? First of all, besides the name "show" that some companies use to define home party, what else does our business have in common with the big screen? Guests at our parties or shows normally spend a minimum of $20 or more—this is about the cost of two people attending a movie. And, movie attendees know they'll be sitting back and entertained for about two hours. So, the common elements are time and money—two things none of us has enough of.

So, how do we show (pun intended) the general public that attending a home party demonstration is not only worth their time and money, but a valuable investment as well? They have to *experience* our great demonstrations. Go back to the reasons why people go to movies...these are the same reasons guests will either want to attend your home party class or not. Let's compare:

1. I know many people love to go to home parties because they can have a "girls night out" for a couple of hours. They know they'll be entertained—not only by the company demonstrator—but also by their friends who are there. In our industry, they'll also be educated in a fun way, if you do your demonstration effectively.

2. Some people are more inclined to attend one company event over others. If you sell kitchen tools, and you have a group of Betty Crocker act-a-likes, they're going to be more receptive to your hostess' invitation than someone who doesn't know a spoon from a spatula. You see, some people are either more attracted or not attracted to your company, depending on their own interests. This is not to say that after attending one of your classes they're not converted to your topic because you gave a dynamic presentation.

3. When a guest receives an invitation or reminder from you or your hostess, and sees your name as the demonstrator (hint: even if your hostess mails out these items, be positive your name and phone number are easily located), is she so excited to attend another one of your presentations because you have such a great reputation for powerful, polished presentations? If the answer to this is not a resounding YES, you can do the *TWIST* and begin holding these kinds of demonstrations using the ideas in this book and by learning from your

leader and others in your company. You want the excitement that comes from seeing your name as the consultant to be like what I feel when I know I'm going to see a new movie with Tom Hanks. And, not only do I go to the movie, but I take a couple of friends. If the guests who are invited by their hostess know you're the demonstrator and love what they've seen you do—or heard about what you do—they'll also take some friends along. Some guests attend solely because of the demonstrator; not because they want more information or product.

4. How do *previews of coming attractions* relate to the party plan industry? When you're at a demonstration, you can tease people by sharing just part of an idea and then stating: "At the next class, I'll give you the rest of the story." Speaking of the rest of the story, I'll give you some more specific examples as we go along on both Featured Attractions and Previews of Coming Attractions.

5. Even more so than movies, bookings in the Home Party Plan industry come more from word of mouth than any other mode of promotion. In fact, that's why companies choose to market a product via the direct sales method. In this way, a company "pays" a hostess with gifts to invite family and friends to her home. Hostesses are rewarded according to the dollars sold and/or new events booked. Additionally, money normally spent on mass advertising can be given to consultants and leaders in the form of commissions and bonuses just for opening their mouths and showing, telling, and selling the product and opportunity. Getting paid for talking— word of mouth advertising—sounds like a great way to make a living. It is. And it's fun.

Some guests attend solely because of the demonstrator; not because they want more information or product.

So, by comparing movies on the big screen with parties in hostesses' homes, what can you as a demonstrator do to entice more people to be more excited to come to more of your presentations more often—*and* bring their friends who will tell their friends who will tell their friends about you, your product, and your wonderful presentations? Long question—short answer: Create *Featured Attractions*—just like they do in the movies!

Many consultants center their classes around a theme; thus they are holding theme parties. Theme parties are a great idea; *Featured Attractions* are even greater. With a theme demonstration, your guests arrive and are wowed by your presentation because it has consistency and flows nicely. The problem is the guests don't really know until they are experiencing the information that they are in for such a treat. With a *Featured Attraction*, the guests and hostess know in advance that they are invited to join a fun, educational, and entertaining event—and they should bring their friends with them. As soon as they are invited, the guests can anticipate your demonstration.

Let's do another *TWIST*. Instead of thinking in the movie terms of "Lights, Camera, Action," think: *BRING, REWARD, RELATE*.

Here's the scenario: You do a top-notch job coaching your hostess on how to personally invite her guests. She's a great hostess, and with all her positive enthusiasm, she calls to invite her sister, Andrea, to her party:

> Liz (Hostess): "Andrea! I am so excited!! I went to a home party with Northrup Party Plan last night. It was fun; the demonstrator was great, and I booked a party of my own for January 21 at 6:30! You're going to love everything there! I can count on you, right?"

> Andrea: "Thanks for calling; but I've already been to one or two of those parties; I don't think I need anything else."

In this dialog, the hostess, Liz, was really excited. She didn't make a big mistake as some hostesses do by saying "You wouldn't want to come to a Northrup Party Plan Party, would you?" No, she was positive. So, what was the big flaw here? She didn't give her sister a reason to come! She didn't show her the value of attending beyond "fun" and "great demonstrator," and "you're going to love it." When guests get an invitation like this, they'll think of going to your party like I feel about going to the mall to shop: "You've seen one, you've seen em' all!" Andrea figured that since she'd attended a couple of the parties and has a few items, why would she need to go again?

When a hostess gets a response like this, she gets discouraged. She did everything you told her so why isn't she getting a better response? Let's do the *TWIST* on the phone call now:

> Liz: "Hi Andrea! You won't believe what I did yesterday! I went to a Super Hero party; it was a blast!!

Andrea: (who now is curious) "What's a Super Hero Party?"

Liz: "You've heard of Northrup Party Plan?"

Andrea: "Yes, I've even been to one or two of the parties and bought a few items....but what does that have to do with being a Super Hero?"

Liz: "Well, I had been to a couple before as well, but none were like this. The demonstrator had everyone bring some thing about a super hero. Since my baby doesn't have any of those action figures, I just took a big towel and told people it was my super hero cape!"

When a hostess invites her guests, she often fails to give a reason for her friends to attend the show.

Andrea: "I don't get it...why would you bring super heroes to a Northrup Party?"

Liz:" I wondered too; if fact that's the only reason I went, because like you, I've been to three or four of these parties. The demonstrator, who was better than any I've seen, taught us how we can make homemade soup really yummy and easy along with hero sandwiches. So, now at dinner, we have a choice: Soup or Heroes!"

Andrea: "Fun!! Tell me more."

Liz: "I don't have time right now, the baby is crying. I was so impressed and learned so much that I decided to have a Northrup party myself; it's going to be on January 21 at 6:30."

Andrea: "Wow, I can't wait. Do I bring something about Super Heroes?"

Liz: "No...I'm actually going to have a Chocoholics Night Out. Just bring your favorite chocolate candy bar!"

Andrea: "Sounds fun; I'll be there. But I really want to know more about those Soup Or Heroes. Do you think the demonstrator would tell me?"

Liz: "I'm sure she'll be busy teaching us chocoholics at my class, but I bet you could book your own Soup Or Hero class from mine."

Andrea: "Maybe I'll do that! Thanks for calling; Go take care of the baby!"

Now, which example sounds best to you? Which scenario makes you wish the party were tomorrow? Are you curious about the Super Hero (Soup Or Hero) concept? What about the Chocoholics Night Out? In this case, Liz was able to give Andrea a great preview of her class, plus entice Andrea with the details of the one Liz just attended. Now, Andrea is likely to book the Soup Or Hero class and she hasn't even met the demonstrator. Are you seeing why the concept is so powerful?

In this situation, Liz was more than excited to invite Andrea. She invited her, gave her a preview of the party, and asked her to *bring* her favorite chocolate bar. Another benefit is that as a consultant, when you have something unique to teach guests, you're more apt to open your mouth and tell everyone what you have to offer. As you read this, don't you want to get on the phone and tell everyone about your Super Hero Party? Keep reading…

Remember, if you're doing the same old same old demonstration time after time, people will know they've seen everything you have to offer. They'll feel like they've seen your movie time after time, and reruns aren't as much fun as something new. If you're not thrilled with what you're going to teach and share, you can believe your guests aren't excited either.

Let's continue on with the example at Liz's show. As guests are arriving at Liz's, the demonstrator, Michelle, meets and greets everyone and sees what kind of chocolate candy bars they are bringing. Important note: Michelle knows that not everyone will remember to bring the candy bars, so she has five or six just in case; she doesn't want anyone to be embarrassed. After the *Introduction*, Michelle gives out the *rewards* for bringing the candy bars. Because she has a good idea of which candy bars the guests have with them, she can create rewards that are relative to the candy bars, so she begins:

Michelle: "Who has a candy bar that is in two pieces (Mounds®, $100,000 Bar, Almond Joy®, etc.)?" She *rewards* the winners with something valuable and inexpensive.

Did anyone bring a candy bar that has nuts, caramel, and chocolate? Appropriate guests get a *reward.*

Is there anyone here whose favorite "candy bar" is really lots of pieces of chocolates like M&Ms or chocolate covered raisins? *Rewards again.*

If you were one of the guests, would you feel honored when you were rewarded? As a consultant, you can choose who and how many people to *reward*. The idea here is to involve the guests, which Michelle did because they all brought something, then she recognized a few, many, or all and presented them with *rewards*. The demonstration has hardly begun and the guests are already glad they are present.

The third key—and this must be done to make a *Featured Attraction* effective—is to *relate the items which were brought to the product and company you're representing*. In other words, you must have a reason for asking the guests to bring their item.

The third key—and this must be done to make a Featured Attraction effective— is to relate the items which were brought to the product and company you're representing.

I've given you a sample of a *Featured Attraction—Chocoholics Night Out*. Can this be related to your product? If you sell rubber stamps, you could blend this in with a demonstration on creating candy bar wrappers. If you sell a kitchen related product, you could let this lead into a presentation on a chocolate recipe. This *Featured Attraction* can work for many companies as long as it relates to your product.

At one of my live Learning Adventures™, I had a group of consultants who represent a company with a line of specialty baskets. They excitedly told me how they use a theme party called "Naughty Nightie." All guests bring an item of clothing that they sleep in placed inside a paper bag. The bags are passed around the room and one at a time the "nighties" are unveiled. The guests then guess who it belongs to.

I've heard this before, and it can be a fun *Featured Attraction*, if you do the *TWIST* and relate it to your product. When I asked the ladies how this related to their baskets, they couldn't answer me, although they did say it was fun! Yet the key to an effective *Featured Attraction* is to relate the item they bring to the product. As a group, we did the *TWIST* and now my basket friends place the bags inside their baskets and then pass the baskets around the room. See how easy that is!

How do you create your own *Featured Attractions*? It begins with your product. If you have the *Lemon Aid Lead Alphabet: Where to Find Customers when you run out of Family and Friends,* you'll remember that the first Lemon Aid Law for Locating Leads is "Know your products so you'll know who your prospects are." I can do a *TWIST* and say, "Know your products so you can create your own Featured Attractions." Simply look at your product, no matter how simple it is, and ask, "How can I build a *Featured Attraction* around this?"

As I was preparing a presentation for a company, I noticed a holder for magazines. My contact told me that a lot of people use that item to store and hide toilet paper in their bathrooms. With that in mind, I created a T-P Party! Everyone brought a roll of toilet paper. We rewarded the one who brought the 2-ply quilted kind as well as those who brought colored T-P. Believe me, people were really curious as to why they were bringing toilet paper, but we had great attendance! We showed how to store T-P out of the way, and then gave other uses for the same product. We ended by putting everyone's "collection" in a big bag and did the grand prize drawing. Guess what the winner took home! See how easy this was?

One thing to keep in mind is that whatever the item is people will be bringing, make sure it's something they probably have at home. If they have to go out and purchase something, they have another reason *not* to attend. Make doing business easy and you'll do more business…and have much more fun.

Throughout your *Featured Attraction* presentation, remember to do *Previews of Coming Attractions*. This is a sneak peek of the other *Featured Attractions* that you offer. I like to do a lot of teasing rather than spending a lot of time (like Hollywood does when you go to a movie). You can also have a portfolio of your *Featured Attractions* for guests to choose from. Even though you might offer dozens and dozens (you'll start creating them quickly and often) of them, I'd only have six to ten to choose from. We all know women. It's so hard to make a choice! But the choice they'll make is to book a *Featured Attraction* with you because they had fun and learned!

Segment Nine

Part of the Action

In the previous segment, I discussed ways of *TWISTING* your home demonstrations into *Featured Attractions*. Did you notice one big difference between the *Featured Attractions* and sitting down in a movie theatre for two-plus hours? The answer is when you're watching a movie, you're not taking part in the action—you're simply a spectator. With a home party *Featured Attraction*, from the onset—the invitation—the guests become involved in the presentation when the hostess asks them to bring something. The guests begin to take *Part of the Action*.

Two of your main goals when you give a demonstration to a group are to sell your company's products and book more events. One vehicle to get more bookings is to make your presentations memorable so that when people remember you (don't forget to use that personal icon), they'll also remember the demonstration.

One way for customers to remember the experience of attending your class is to allow them to touch and use your products and then to teach others.

How guests Remember

How do you present memorable, never-to-be-forgotten demonstrations? Let me share a study about *recall*. When we read something we remember only 10% of what we read. So, if you rely solely on book parties—where people simply look at a catalog and place an order—they'll only remember 10% of what they *read*. The bottom line is, they won't purchase as much, and more importantly, they won't fully understand the features, benefits, and value of what they do purchase.

Recall doubles to 20% when we *hear* something. This is where word of mouth comes in to play. If someone tells her friend about your nifty gadget, the friend will remember the gadget more than if she simply saw it in your company catalog. If you have someone who will only do a "book party" encourage her to tell her friends about her experiences with some of your products.

When we actually *see* something—like seeing your products at a home demonstration—the rate of remembering increases to 30%. Couple the action of hearing with seeing and people will retain 50%. In the world of parties, when a guest sees an item at your demonstration she's three times more likely to remember it than if she simply saw it in a catalog. However, if you demonstrate the product so she's hearing information about it, her memory increases dramatically.

After a guest has seen and heard you explain the nifty gadget, and another guest arrives late to the show, and the first guest explains the nifty gadget to the second person, the first person will remember 80% of what she told the second person. That's because we remember 80% of what we say or teach.

It gets better. When you allow the guest to come up and try out the nifty gadget and then she demonstrates the nifty gadget to someone else, she will remember 90% of what she says as she acts! Since you've been a consultant with your company, haven't you learned the most by teaching customers at your shows?

We all know most people do not buy everything they want at our classes. After your guests return home and a couple of weeks have gone by, don't you want them to remember the items you demonstrated? One way for customers to remember the experience of attending your class is to allow them to touch and use your products and then to teach others.

Testimonials

That brings me to one of the ways to have guests take part in the action is to let them give testimonials (where have you heard that before?) to others. In other words, your demonstration is not a classroom where you are the teacher and the guests are the students, and you want the students to be quiet while you teach. Rather, do the *TWIST*: encourage guests to touch the products and share their experiences with the group. Believe me, guests will listen to and believe other guests more than they'll listen to and believe you. Your goal should be to have the role as a facilitator, not a dictator.

Learn from Guests

Encouraging this kind of interaction helps you learn more about the features and benefits of your products. Guests will share ideas you've never thought of or heard! And when you go to another show and share the ideas you learned from your previous guests, you will become a great resource—a "tower of wisdom" as my good friend Ruth says! When you allow guests to take part in your teaching, you'll also be able to identify those who are at ease talking and sharing. These are the perfect prospects for your future team.

Involve the Senses

Another way to increase learning and recall is to involve as many senses as you can. If you represent a company focusing on food, and you teach cooking classes or have sampling sessions, use the powerful sense of taste. If your product has a fragrance, allow people to sample the smells. The more senses you involve, the more dollars you'll make!

One caution in both of these examples is to be sure people don't have allergies to food or to the fragrance. You don't want involving the senses to backfire!

The more senses you involve, the more dollars you'll make!

Illustration of Participation

When giving your presentation, ask yourself if the guests could be taking part in the action. I worked with a friend who was a consultant for The Pampered Chef®. In teaching her this technique, we made my favorite brownie concoction as a group effort. Everyone sat around the hostess' large kitchen table. The consultant first placed a pan of already-baked brownies in the middle. We had everyone wash their hands (very important when cooking) using one of the company's products. Then, as a group, we added the finishing touches. We distributed the different tools...one person mixed the creamy mixture in the batter bowl and used the scraper. The next person sliced the bananas with the egg slicer; another person sampled the knife and cutting board as she sliced strawberries. Another guest chopped peanuts with the food chopper; the person next to her grated chocolate as a garnish.

The dessert had its own personality! It wasn't as picture perfect as if the consultant had done it all herself; after all she had a lot of practice! But the guests loved that they were taking part of the action; not simply listening to a lecture.

Many party plan companies are activity-based—from stamping cards to applying make up to creating scrap book pages to trying on outfits and jewelry. Isn't this another benefit of having people attend a home party rather than browsing through a retail store? You probably have figured out that things can get a bit rowdy when everyone is participating. Yet, you can still be in control in most cases.

I have had to concede when I simply could not get the group's attention. The few times this did occur, it was not when people were involved; it was when they were simply sitting and listening to my *lecture* (before I figured this out). Guests will normally chit chat with one another when they are bored. Inviting them to take part in the action eliminates the boredom. You might recall the ancient Chinese proverb: "I hear and I forget, I see and I remember, I do and I understand."

Actively draw your guests and hostesses into your presentations in as many ways as possible. And more and more guests will understand not only how and why they need your products, but also that the best way to be serviced by you is to attend your informative demonstrations rather than just ordering from a catalog.

Segment Ten

The Power of Props

As I illustrated in the last segment, having guests take part of the action at your presentations increases bookings because they become involved. Adding some props—or visuals—to your demo expands their involvement and desire to see and hear more of your ideas, and thus agree to more bookings. Remember, the key in marketing a product and business opportunity is to get prospects remembering you and your company. Studies have shown that when you "show *and* tell," not just show or not just tell, people can recall 85% of the information three hours after they heard it, and 65% of information three days after hearing it.

Props are simple decorations or products that you use to attract attention or questions and to explain your product or opportunity.

Seasonal Props

When you walk through retail stores from September to December, you're likely to see Halloween, Harvest, and Christmas decorations on display. In early Spring, the décor is flowers and sunshine. Obviously you can use similar ornamentations at your shows; they do make your display more appealing.

What I want to teach you in this segment is to do more than decorate your display, but rather to use props for more profit! In this way, props are simple decorations or products that you use to attract attention or questions and to explain your product or opportunity.

Let's talk about how to use seasonal props. In the months of March and April, I use the plastic fill and thrill Easter eggs. Most people will use them only to embellish a display. I'm going to teach you how to use them to add more bookings and recruits. Inside each egg, I put the name of a product that will be demonstrated or a hint I want to share along with a wrapped piece of candy (people love something to eat; just be sure it's wrapped!). I like using the Nestle® Nest Eggs. In one or two of the plastic eggs, I put a piece of candy that is wrapped in gold foil.

After guests have been seated, I pass the eggs around and ask each guest to take at least one. I normally use 12-15, so sometimes guests can take two, depending on how many people are in attendance. I have them examine the egg without opening it, then I ask the guests if they have a sufficient nest egg for their retirement. If the answer if "no" which it is likely to be, I quickly explain that earning $200 a month from working part time in the company (that normally translates to only two or three classes a month), would add $2,400 a year to an IRA. When adding each year along with interest, just a few hours a month would add substantially to their nest egg.

This is probably a different approach than you've heard used before. Most consultants talk about the here and now—needing extra money for school clothes, vacations, or just time away from the kids. See, I did the *TWIST* here, and I'll attract more people because I'm future-minded. Why? Because I planted a seed (an egg is a seed) for joining my team in a very practical, non-threatening, customer-focused way! My goal is to have them think of my opportunity every time they see one of these plastic eggs.

Next, I allow each guest to crack open the egg they are holding. I randomly choose people to read the slip of paper they've found in their egg; eventually everyone has a chance to share what was in her egg. When the slips with the names of products are read, I take the opportunity to demonstrate that product. If the slip of paper has a tip or an announcement, I share that. For example, on one of the slips I write down *delivery date*. When a guest reads this I announce the approximate date that the order will be sent to the hostess. Another slip might say *ways to pay*. This is when I explain the check (and to whom it is written), cash, and credit card payments. In other words, the group does my entire demonstration. I've involved them, they laugh, they listen, they book!

What about the "golden eggs?" Whoever is the holder of these eggs is honored with a special packet of information about the company. This might be a brochure, company magazine, or audio tape. I only give this to the "golden eggs." I watch the faces of other guests who might be curious or disappointed because they didn't get the golden egg and the information. I can always talk to those persons individually.

Out of Season Props

In the last example, I shared an idea for springtime. Now, let's do another *TWIST*. What would the reaction of your audience be if you had a basket of eggs and used this idea in September? Most people are expecting that you'll be talking about fall and back to school. If you liked the last idea in using props for participating in the demonstration as well as attracting new team members, why not use it at other times of the year? You know, people thing of their retirement nest egg year round. In fact, because you are *different* rather than like all the other party plan consultants who have not read this book, people will remember you! And when you use seasonal props with a *TWIST*, you'll be remembered.

Taking Props Home

Early on as a home party consultant, I learned people should always take three things away from a demonstration: something for their *heart*—the feeling that they enjoyed themselves and want to come back again or book their own show; something for their *head*—information that they are glad they know and know how to use; and something for their *hand*—this can be a prop, your business card, literature, or anything else that is very valuable-yet-inexpensive.

By far, the best prop is your product.

Have you ever planned a child's birthday party? The highlight for the party guests is to take home their treat bag. What kind of a treat are you giving out at your shows that people want to take home to use and keep? I believe your catalog is something they want to take home; this will be discussed in the next segment. Beyond that, think of something inexpensive and valuable.

Guests could take home a plastic Easter egg with your business card information on a label simply affixed to the egg. Maybe you have a fun tip or recipe that you've printed up on a card for everyone to take home. Bookmarks with a *TWIST* are nice giveaways, and people always love magnets. Jenny B, The Booster, has a great assortment, and they're very valuable yet inexpensive. Have you done something fun with your business card to reinforce your personal icon? Give one to each guest. These little touches make a remarkable, memorable difference.

Products as Props

Again, I've saved the best idea for last. You can buy little trinkets or decorations and they can be effective for teaching, selling, and recruiting. By far, the best prop is using your product. I look at product lines and, while doing a mental *TWIST*, think how can I use these props to tell a story. Sometimes the story I want to tell is about my business opportunity. This is one of the best ways to attract the attention of possible recruits. Sometimes I use the props to tell a story and teach ideas on using the product and prop. Because this book is written for the general Party Plan industry, I won't be specific. However, when I come to your group or company to speak, request me to do a story with props just for you. You can also get some ideas during my Lemon Aid One-on-One consulting service.

Paper Potential

Tradition has it that paperwork is a lot of *work*. This might be true in some industries, but in direct sales, paper has a powerful potential to multiply our profits—if we use these paper tools correctly. This segment discusses some important pieces of paper: order forms, the *Getting to Know More About You* drawing slip, Guest Register, the company catalog, the *Hostess Presentation Package*, and recruiting literature. Keep in mind this book was written for the entire party plan industry. Your particular company might have other powerful pieces of paper that can be incorporated into these ideas.

The Order Form

Before I wrote my first book, I wanted to know more about the book selling industry, so I worked part-time in a retail bookstore. I learned that people love books and buy a lot. I also noticed that people would probably buy more if they had a shopping basket or cart. But when their arms were full, and they grew tired of carrying their purchases, they came to the check out. I mentioned this to the store manager who just shrugged his shoulders and mentioned something about baskets being too cumbersome to take care of. He was more concerned about his duties than the customers' needs.

Contrast this to entering WalMart®. When I walk in, what does the door greeter give me? A shopping cart! A couple of times I've declined the cart; after all, I only needed a head of lettuce and a loaf of bread. Sure enough, every time I'd hike back to the store entrance to get a cart because along the way, I discovered other things I had to have. Now, I always take a cart. And, yes, I do buy more than I planned. What if the greeter told me to walk around and look at everything, and then come and get a cart and check out, would I end up buying much? I might even forget to get the couple items I came for. What would I do if I had a huge list of things to buy?

In the Party Plan industry, we also need to provide our customers with a shopping cart—our *order form*. This way, people will actually order from us, and not simply "window shop" through the catalog. I believe in placing an order form or a copy of the order form in every catalog that you give or mail to customers. At our demonstrations, we always provide order forms, so why not include a shopping cart every time you distribute your catalog, even if they are not at a demonstration?

Some order forms can be confusing when tax, shipping, and handling need to be added. If the tax is figured on where you as the consultant are based, fill in the tax rate on the order form so the customer will know what rate to use. If you collect tax based on where the order will be shipped—normally the customer's address—write in the tax rate for her city. Additionally, include a shipping chart or highlight a chart if it is printed on your catalog. If shipping is based on a percentage, write that amount next to the word "shipping" on the order form. The bottom line is, the easier you make doing business with you, the more business you will do. If a customer can easily figure out the order form herself, calculate the amount in addition to shipping and handling, and taxes, the more orders you'll get.

The easier you make doing business with you, the more business you will do.

On the other hand, for people using credit cards for purchases, figuring out their totals to the exact penny isn't as crucial. If they have an idea of what they'll be charged and can figure the cost out if they choose to, they are happier customers.

Order Forms at Parties

As a member of nearly every hotel "frequent stayer" club, I love the one special perk I get when I check in: My room key card folder is in a special, plastic see-through wall holder reserved just for the frequent stayers. The reservation is already processed. I know they've been expecting me and I feel like a VIP. How can we give our party guests the same welcome feeling that they are very important persons when they arrive?

First, you have to get a completed guest list back from the hostess. Refer to Segment One of this book, *Pre-Presentation* for more details on guest lists. If your company provides the mailing list, great! If not, use the one provided at the back of this book. Next, create labels with each person's name, address, and phone number. I simply use the label template in Microsoft® Works program. Creating this does not take much time. And, as you type the names, you become familiar with them. And when you get to the presentation, you're simply matching names with faces; therefore, you can call people by name, and they are so surprised!

Print out three copies of the mailing labels, one for the mailer (if you have a company-provided mailing list, you would not need to have this copy unless the handwriting is difficult for the post office to read), one for the order forms, and a set to take to the class. A label on the order form? Yes, this is the *TWIST*. The second set of labels will be used to put on each person's order form. You'll keep these order forms and the third set of labels in the valuable file folder where you store the guest list (refer to the *Pre-Presentation* segment).

When you go to the demonstration, you'll take these personalized order forms with you. As you *meet and greet* each guest, you will present her with this personalized gift—the order form that is waiting for her, complete with her name, address, and phone number. What does this convey—rather than out right say? It conveys: "I've been expecting you." Don't we all like to think people have been awaiting our presence? Sure we do. We all like to feel wanted and appreciated. Another benefit is the guest doesn't have to write out all this information—you've done the work for her. All she has to do is order! And, she'll probably feel more like ordering when you've made the task simple for her! The easier you make doing business with you, the more business you'll do.

I know you have some questions about this terrific *TWIST*. Let me answer them before you can ask:

What happens if the people don't come?
This technique is great because after the show, when you're sitting down with your host to review the sales, simply hand her the order forms and explain these are the people she invited who did not attend. You already have the order forms started, all she has to do is call the people to get their orders. She might even have some pre-party orders from those guests so you only have to transfer the information onto the order forms. Think how easy it will be for her to call her guests for an order; all the information is ready.

What if they don't come or order? Won't I be wasting a lot of order forms?
If the hostess doesn't use the order forms, she can return them to you. You won't waste them as you can always place another label on top.

If I only put one label on the order form, but my order form has three copies, what do I do?
The bottom copy is normally given to the guest that evening. She probably doesn't care that her name isn't on it. The middle copy is usually left with the hostess for packing the order. Bring the third set of labels (this is why you initially print out three sets) to put on the hostess' copy. Of course, every company and order form is different, but you should be able to adapt easily with these suggestions.

What if someone comes who was not listed on the guest list?
Personally write in her information for her. When you *ink it, not just think it*, you'll remember her name.

The best benefit of *pre-labeling* is your guests will feel special. And when they feel special, they will want a repeat performance from you—they'll schedule a workshop and won't question you when you ask for a guest list to be returned because they will have experienced the benefits and will want their guests to do the same. Another benefit is you'll actually be able to read the names on the order forms! Sometimes people write quickly and sloppily.

The Best Things to Order

What is the most important item your guests can order on your order form? YOU! You want all your guests to order *you*. Look closely on your company order form. You'll probably see some boxes where customers can indicate if they want to book a class or sell the product. Do you ever look at these boxes?

The most important item your guests can order on your order form is YOU!

I never paid close attention to them in the beginning of my career because I didn't have the self-confidence to know if people were sure they wanted to hire me to come to their home. So I ignored the boxes. Until I got a call from a lady who wondered why I hadn't called her to get a date for her party. When I apologized for not knowing she wanted to be a hostess, she explained that she had "checked the box." From then on, so did I!

In fact, not only did I check the checks in the box, I made a big deal about "circling the boxes." Instead of casually mentioning, "Oh, by the way, if you want to book a show or sell my product, check one of these boxes," I did a real *TWIST*. Here is a script that I used:

> "Ladies, as you place your order tonight, consider ordering the best, most unique product available: ME coming to teach YOU even more about…(this is where you give a preview of Coming Attractions). If you want to order ME, take a look at the line on the order form that says, 'I'm interested in scheduling my own party.' What that box really means is 'I enjoyed myself so much tonight that I want all my friends to come to my house and learn more about _____
> (company name) and while I'm inviting my friends, I want to earn the special hostess gifts.'
> "You see, there wasn't enough room to write the

complete *definition*. And, please *don't check* the box. Instead, *draw a great big circle around that sentence!* This way, I'll know right away to look for a place to circle you on my calendar."

Here's a *TWIST* for the recruiting box:

"Ladies if after making the list of all the products you want, you've run out of space—and maybe out of money—then we have another payment option you can take advantage of.

Please note the box that says 'I want more information about starting my own home-based business.' Well, *what this really means is*, I love _____ (company name) so much that I'd rather *get paid* for telling others about the great items than *paying* for all the things I want. Please give me information immediately about being on the best team in _____ (company name)." Remember, *please don't check the box*; put a great big circle *and* a great big star *and* dollar sign next to this sentence because you're going to be the next star on my team who will be making big bucks!"

Are these statements a bit embellished? You bet they are! And, they'll get the attention of your guests. Really tease them about "not checking" the boxes. Teach them if they'll make circles, they'll eventually be earning dollars and/or gifts! Let the order form work for you!! It's definitely the "shopping cart" for your customers and a "bank account" for you!

Getting to Know More about You

I remember when Door Prize Drawing slips made their entrance in to the party plan world. As consultants and leaders we thought: "What a concept; we'll no longer have to ask people to date classes; they'll just check the box." I learned early on that like anything in life, this was not a magic formula. And as a guest at many home parties, I sometimes wonder how effective the drawing slips are in building a business—especially when they are typically handed out at the end of a presentation and often the drawing is an after thought by the consultant as people are leaving. This doesn't have a lot of impact.

The other thing I dislike about this medium is that I got many false positives and positive negatives. Meaning, a person checked "yes" on a box (a positive response) and yet when I asked her for a date, she was negative about being a hostess. Or, some people were positive they didn't want to be a hostess so they automatically marked "no" on every box without really reading the statements. Just for the fun of it, I've often thought of adding a statement that says: "If I win the lottery, I want a lump-sump check to go to my _____ (company name) consultant." You should try that once in a while; what you'll find is a lot of people never read those statements on the slips—so why use them? How about using a slip with a *TWIST*.

We all know the reason we use the slips is to book and recruit—even our customers know this! And if our order forms have essentially the same recruiting and booking questions/statements and you're now about to learn some *TWISTS* on using that tool, isn't using these slips a bit redundant and a waste of our paper and our customers' time?

Additionally, every company will have different reasons for attracting hostesses—the reasons why someone books a demonstration with a skin care company will differ from the reasons someone books with a scrapbook business. So, why is everyone using such similar door prize slips? All that I've seen have essentially the same information.

Let's customize a *Getting to Know More About You* slip for your individual company, one which focuses on your customers—not on how many more bookings and sales you can get; those results come when we become customer-centered. And, let's begin by changing the name. "Door prize drawing" connotes one person is going to get a big prize. You'll see the *TWIST* on the "prize" as well. The name will depend on the name of your company and the category of products you sell. If your product is kitchen related, you could title this, "What's Cooking with You?" If you sell toys or products directed to children, "The Child in You" might be appropriate. If you sell home décor and gifts, perhaps "What's under your Roof" would work. The decision is yours. Whatever you call this, the object is to get to know more about your customers in a short amount of time, and to use this information to show the guest how you can solve any *Sour Situations* she has and to add to her *Sweet Successes*.

Filling out this slip must be very simple and quick for the guests. You only want her name—no address and phone is needed, as you'll see. When I've been a guest, I've sometimes felt like I was applying for a mortgage on my house as I filled out so many pieces

Customize a Getting to Know More About You slip for your individual company, one which focuses on your customers—not on how many more bookings and sales you can get; those results come when we become customer-centered.

of paper (this is another reason why I like using the pre-labeled order forms). What I'm looking for are the person's interests and hobbies and to see how they relate to my product and service.

Under the line where her name is written, I write, "Please circle the activities you love to do." Under this I list appropriate activities or interests such as: shop, cook, eat, decorate, garden, work, read, soak in the bath tub, create crafts, go to movies, hang out with my friends. I list about a half-dozen more "Circle responses…" that somehow apply to my product/company. More "circle responses" can be:

Work Full Time   Work Part Time   Mom/Dad of ___ kids

I also put in a couple "fill in the blanks" with responses that will relate to my product or service. For example: Favorite Fragrance (for companies who sell perfumes), Favorite Season of the year (rubber stamp/scrapbook companies), Favorite Color to Wear (clothing, lingerie, jewelry companies), Favorite food (food or kitchen related companies), Favorite Sport (wellness companies). You can list three of four of these "favorites"

Some of these ideas can *cross-over*. If you sell clothing, you might want to know their favorite sport so they can purchase appropriate outfits. The "favorites" can also *indirectly relate* to your products. For example, ask for their favorite restaurant, favorite magazine, or favorite vacation destination.   When you assist them with their order, you can begin "customer-focused" conversations:

> "Penny, I notice your favorite restaurant is Fogo De Chão. Isn't that Brazilian food the best? Have you ever lived in Brazil? We have some friends from Brazil; do you know _____?"

Can you see how you'll be able to find commonalities that connect along with her wants and needs as you begin to converse? Maybe they know my Brazilian friends. I can then suggest she host a class with me and invite our mutual friends. She might say how much she loves the restaurant, but can only afford to dine their once a year; here's an opportunity to mention earning extra cash for the extras in life.

I also have a *fill in the blank* for "I've attended _____ classes." With this statement, leave one blank line so they fill in how many events they've attended. The second blank is where you'll fill in the name of your company so it reads: "I've attended _____ Creative Memories Classes." And another *fill in*: "I've hosted _____ parties." Again, leave a line for the guest to write in the number she's hosted. The second blank is for you to write in the name of your company: "I've hosted_____ Tupperware Parties."

I like to know the months of my guests' birthdays; on the form I write: "My birthday is in _____." The last line on this slip is: "Please keep me updated on products/specials: Monthly Quarterly Annually" Guests circle their choice. Now I know how often to contact them and I have their permission to do so.

Remember the reason I want to do a *TWIST* on the door-prize drawing slips is to make this *easy* for my guests. I've just given you a few ideas here; don't turn this into an ACT/SAT college entrance exam! Choose a *few* that are appropriate to you and your company. Creating a *Customize Slip* for you, your company, and your customers is a service I offer through Speaking and Consulting.

When do you distribute these slips? At the beginning of the class. Have guests complete and return them right away. Now, throughout the presentation, I'll pull a slip and say something like: "This person has a birthday in May; if your birthday is in May, raise your hand." If only one person raises her hand, she's obviously the one. However, if more than one has listed a May birthday, when they raise their hands, they look at the others with May birthdays. You'll hear comments such as: "I didn't know you were a May baby," or "What day is your birthday?" Guests begin to connect with each other, and the best part: You get to know more about your guests. And they feel honored as you recognize them.

The real value in using these slips is when you assist people with their order. You can quickly review their *Getting to Know More about You* form. If you see they've circled "shop," "eat," and "hang out with friends" as some of their "love to do activities," now you can invite them to be a hostess by saying:

"Julie, looks like you and your friends love to shop, eat, and hangout! Did you enjoy shopping, eating, and hanging out at our party tonight? (She responds.) Next month, I'm offering a Chocoholics Night Out _____ (your company name) Party; how would you like me to bring those ideas and products to your home?" (In place of "Chocoholics Night Out," you can insert the name of another Featured Attraction that's applicable to your company.)

The real value in using these slips is when you assist people with their order. You'll be able to see how you can add value to her interests, hobbies, and family with your products and opportunity.

This is just one example of many dialogs you can have with potential hostesses as you review information about them and about what they love to do. With this data, you'll be able to recognize guests throughout your presentation (much better than an "after thought drawing") and match what they like to the products and services you offer as you add more bookings to your book and recruits to your team!

Guest Register

In the segment on *Name Game* under the subtitle of "Cheat Sheet" I taught you how to create a Guest Register and promised more information; here it is. Have you ever had guests come to a party, listen intently to your presentation, and then leave with the words, "I'll call with my order later."? Most have good intentions to call, but life happens. Or, you've met a guest who seems quite interested in booking a class. She's asking a lot of questions and gets real excited when you show hostess gifts. Then, her beeper goes off and she has to leave to go to work. In another scenario, an invited guest brings a friend along to the party who you are really impressed with. But before you can visit with either of them, they leave. Last example: the guests at your party think they are saving on shipping and handling so they combine their orders.

In each of the situations I've just described, how are you going to connect with these people to place an order, book a class, find more information on your business, or simply have a phone number for customer service calls?   Remember, they haven't placed an order, so you have no contact information for them.

If your hostess gave you a guest list, you probably have the names and phone numbers on the list and can call them. Thank heavens for guest lists! But wait: what about the times you don't have a guest list, or the example where the guest was brought as a friend? The answer is the *Guest Register*. When people autograph your book, you have their contact information. This is why, if there were only one mode for collecting guests' information, it would be the *Guest Register*. Remember, I have her name pre-printed on a label for her order form. All I want on her *Getting to Know More About You* form is her name. Now, autographing my *Guest Register* is the only time she really has to write her name, phone, and address.

I'll explain what to do if someone hesitates to autograph my book. First, remember how I positioned this by referring back to the *Name Game* segment under "Cheat Sheet." I presented it as a special opportunity to be in attendance and to sign my book. Now, if someone balks at my request, no big deal! Only once did someone question me about this, and that's because she thought she was signing up to have a party. I teasingly replied, "No, people are my hostesses by invitation only, not by autographing my book." Not only did she register in my book, she was the first to book after she had experienced my demonstration.

Additionally, I usually end my presentation by doing a fun recognition and reward for those in my *Guest Register*. I count how many people autographed; let's say there were nine. I'd turn to the hostess (without her knowing where I got the "magic number"), and say: "Jane, can you tell me a magic number between one and nine?" She says: "Six." Now, I count down—or up—six names. I see that it's Margo. I announce: "Margo autographed our Magic Number line!" I present her with something very inexpensive and valuable, and then say: "Since Jane [the hostess] chose the Magic Number, Margo, do you think we should reward her as well?" Of course she says "yes" and I recognize and reward Margo as well. As guests see that you're using your *Guest Register* for this purpose, when they attend future classes of yours they'll more fully understand the concept.

Names are worth millions!

In the *Name Game* segment I explained how the *Guest Register* is a cheat sheet for remembering names. However, let me tell you other ways that this has much more potential for profit. First, and probably the most important reason, is that I have a record of everyone who attended the show. This way, I can connect with my guests even if they don't order, leave early, or come with a friend. Remember, names are worth millions! What if the lady who left early because her beeper went off joins your team *because* you were able to follow through *because* you had her name in your Guest Register? What if she becomes your next leader? What if she becomes one of the top money earners in the company—never having to be attached to an employer's beeper again! So this is the most important reason for collecting this data.

After I've collected all the orders, next to each guest's name, I write down her before-tax/handling/shipping amount (the total hostess gifts are based on), and next to that total the amount the guest needs to pay. If I've collected the money, I indicate that with a code of *ck* for check, *cs* for cash, or *cc* for credit card. This way, I can easily identify those who have not paid and whose money the hostess needs to gather. Most importantly, I can easily add up the hostess amount so she knows where she stands with regard to her gifts and how many more orders and/or bookings (if any) she needs to get. Always give this information to the hostess before you leave. She deserves to know the results. If she gave me advance orders, I include this on the *Guest Register* and also add any that come in after the class. Yes, I do write these names in with my own handwriting; thus, I can easily see that these people ordered but did not attend—great prospects for future bookings.

The *Guest Register* also gives me a chronological system for keeping track of my parties. Sometimes I'll remember Gina from a party, but I can't remember what party I met her at. I do recall that it was around Easter time because she was just leaving for spring break. So, I simply turn to the pages of my guest register from March and April and look for Gina's name.

The *Guest Register* is also a backup copy of all customers who attended and placed an order at demonstrations. If one of my files is misplaced (a nice way of saying lost), I have a cross reference way of keeping track of my database. I have a phobia about losing any kind of information—customers' names or my favorite recipes—so I always put the information in more than one place.

Recruiting with the Guest Register

The last reason really has the most long-term results because it is a way to recruit with your *Guest Register*. When you're interviewing people for your team and explain "the average demonstration and average profit" how can you show your personal profit picture? With the *Guest Register*. When I'm interviewing you, I use my company literature and my guest register. Keep in mind that my *Guest Register* is actually written by all my customers and hostesses—it's in their own handwriting. I haven't neatly typed or printed any statistics—or made any of the names up! Now, as I want to show a profit picture to you as a prospect, I don't need to rely on averages and figures from my company. I simply thumb through my guest register where I have written the total sales of each party.

Here's how our conversation will go:

> "Shanna, the average sales at our home parties is $400. From that amount, your profit will be 25%--or $100. To show you actual demonstrations, let's look at my guest register [thumb through your book as you explain the following]. This show at Bobbie's was quite a bit above average, it was $861.00; my profit was $215 for those two hours. Now, this next one at Tami's

was right at $402; very average. Debbie's was a $568, and look at Kim's; while we had a great time, her sales were $211—below the average—but I met Jessie and Jenny and their shows were $780 and $519 respectively and I dated three parties from each of theirs. I've shown you just the six classes I've done in the past three weeks. My profits were more than $800, I held six classes—total time was less than 15 hours—and had 14 new bookings."

Again, I can read minds. You're saying: "But I haven't held six classes yet; how can I do this?" The answer: start holding more classes. From these classes you're going to find the prospects to talk to. The more people you talk to the more bookings you'll have, the more prospects, and the more recruits—using this simple idea that will benefit you in many areas.

Cash-a-Log, Catalog

Your company catalogs are a wonderful example of an inexpensive tool that is very valuable—whether you buy your catalogs for pennies or dollars. I realize a few companies have such comprehensive catalogs, they are actually *how to* or *recipe books* for using their products. In this case, the catalogs are actually purchased by guests for $6.00-$10.00; a great investment! Catalogs are called by a variety of names from wish book, to showcase, to product reference guide. They all have one thing in common—they contain pictures, prices, and descriptions of a company's products. *And with your name and phone number included.* While a picture's worth a thousand words, catalogs, when used properly can be worth many thousands in sales when coupled with an effective product demonstration and catalog presentation.

While a picture's worth a thousand words, catalogs, when used properly can be worth many thousands in sales when coupled with an effective product demonstration and catalog presentation.

When do you hand catalogs out to guests? How do you present and position your catalog when handing it to a customer? Do you give out catalogs, or insist that guests return them before leaving? Do you recycle your catalogs? How do you convince your guests, who do take your catalog home, to hold on to the catalog and refer to it often? How can catalogs be the book that will put more bookings in your book?

When to Hand out catalogs

Let's answer one question at a time. First, when is the best time to give catalogs to guests? The answer depends on you, really. I've met many consultants who fear if a guest has a catalog in hand, she won't pay attention to the demonstration. Thus, these consultants wait until the end of the demonstration. If you are teaching concepts that must have absolute undivided attention and the catalog would detract from that, using catalogs at the end might be best.

Personally, I like to do what the guests want. When you attend a home party demonstration as a guest, when do you like to have a catalog in hand? I think every guest is dying to delve into a catalog when they arrive. During the time when you hand the catalog out and when you begin a demonstration, a guest can already decide on several items she wants. Guests also begin chatting to each other about what they have and want to buy. They begin encouraging each other to purchase their own favorite items. Some guests, as I'll be teaching you very soon, will be bringing back their catalogs to your class. Those who don't have one of their own will want one now. Further, if your demonstration is well-planned and presented, listening to you will be more appealing than looking at things on paper. If life were perfect (and I know it's not), my choice is to present the catalog on arrival.

The catalog can also be used as an important part of your presentation. If you're doing a cooking demonstration and the recipe is in the catalog, the guests can more easily follow along and will have fewer questions. I also like to do a *catalog clue* activity to familiarize the guests with the catalog. I might ask: "Who can find the picture of the three lemons on a plate?" While they are looking for the lemons, they discover other items they might not normally find.

A few years ago, I attended a craft-based home party. The demonstrator did not want us to have catalogs in advance. Yet, throughout her presentation, she'd refer to her own catalog and point to pictures of items she didn't have with her. I couldn't figure out what the difference was—looking at her catalog that I really couldn't see, or one of my own in my hand so that I could have actually seen the items she referenced. Sometimes, as consultants, we want total control over a demonstration. We have to decide if we can give up control to a catalog that will produce cash.

Presenting the Catalog

At some point of the demonstration, I do a grand catalog presentation. I begin by asking:

> "Is there anyone here who has ever read a best seller?" A few hands go up and I continue, "You are holding a best seller in your hands right now—the _____ (company name) catalog. For a product to make it in this catalog, the

product must be a best seller! Not only is this a best seller with best-selling products, but it also has the name of the best seller in the company here on the back cover (or wherever your contact information is)…it's me!"

Tell your guests that you are the Best Seller! You have to believe it. You are the best seller. I didn't say the highest, but you are the best! If you don't believe this, discover why you're not and do the *TWIST*. I'm confident that as you become aware of improving your presentations (reading and implementing the ideas in this book is a great start), your bookings will improve and you'll progress. Further, look in the mirror and say: "I am the Best!" and become the best. In doing this, you might just become the highest sales person as well! Soon, your customers will be telling their friends that you are the best!

Tell your guests that you are the Best Seller! You have to believe it. You are the best seller. I didn't say the highest, but you are the best! If you don't believe this, discover why you're not and do the TWIST.

By the way, your contact information should not be handwritten. Purchase a rubber stamp with at least your name and phone number. If you want to add address, fax, e-mail, website, that's fine. If you're not into *inking*, use labels or stickers with this data. This is a simple touch of professionalism

Let me show you some highlights of the catalog. First, have your guests turn to the Centerfold! Now you have the guests' attention. Most catalogs are stapled and will easily fall open to the center. Examine your catalog. What is in the center? I love when companies have their hostess programs and specials right in the middle – the centerfold. Whatever your center is, highlight it. When you do, people will laugh, and when they laugh, they listen.

If your catalog is full of hints and tips, point them out. These add value. Also focus on the pages that explain your business opportunity. Introduce the guests to consultants whose names, stories, and pictures appear throughout. And, if you're a *catalog gal* yourself (someone who is featured in the catalog), you need to make a really, really big deal about that—and congratulations from me on that accomplishment! In fact, I'd love to have an autographed copy of the company catalog with your picture and/or story for my collection. Please send it to The Lemon Aid Lady, P.O. Box 1720, Lake Dallas TX 75065.

Take-home Catalogs
If guests purchase your catalog, show them other valuable, informative pages and let them know the catalog costs *only* $____ . If you are willing to give your catalog away, announce that they are welcome to take the catalog home so long as they don't decorate the trash

can with its pages. This is a nice way of implying: "If you don't want to keep it, don't take it."

Next, tell them where their catalog wants to live" in their home. If your product is lingerie and sleepwear, tell them, "Your catalog wants to live in your lingerie drawer." If you sell kitchen tools, suggest having the catalog "live with your cookbooks." If you sell skin care, the catalog should live in a vanity drawer. In other words, what will the guests be doing and where will they be when they think of needing to order more items from you? That's where they need to store their catalog. If I'm low on cleanser for my face, I don't want to have to hunt down the company catalog in a stack of magazines in the family room. Neither will your customers. Also, when they store the catalog next to where they use the product, they'll think of you over and over.

Autograph, Recycle, and *Book*

I love to have my guests use the catalogs *they* recycle; read this carefully as this is one of my favorite *TWISTS*. As I'm doing the catalog presentation, I inform those who want to take care of the catalog and take it to live in their home, that I'll *personally* autograph the catalog next to my name stamp/sticker. Here is a sample text:

"Ladies, if you were at a bookstore and saw a stack of best selling books—some were naked and the others were autographed—which one would you want? Tonight, I'll be happy to autograph your best seller. And, when you bring the catalog back to two more parties and collect a total of three of my autographs, I'll give you something special to take home."

(You choose what this item will be; remember something valuable and inexpensive).

I created my autograph game so that my guests would bring their catalogs back to the parties. Thus, they were using catalogs that they themselves had recycled. And it worked! Instead of giving the same people new catalogs over and over, they were bringing the catalogs back. In between attending classes, they had my catalog for additional ordering. But something even better resulted...

People were actually excited to collect my autograph! At first I wanted to laugh! I didn't think my autograph would be something anyone would want—except for my monthly bill collectors on my check. Here's the best part: When I announced the "collect three autographs," I noticed that two or three guests would huddle together to converse. Then they'd call me over. "Hey, Christie, do you have Wednesday, the 2nd open? I'll do a class that night and Shelley [she points to another guest in her huddle] will do one on the 28th. That way we'll both have three autographs!"

Now, when this happens—and it will—don't act like "I can't believe booking classes is so easy!" Trust me, when I first started doing this, I wanted to jump up and down—it was so simple and fun! Instead, gracefully and professionally take your calendar over to the group, act like this happens all the time, and secure the dates. This really does work. And, can you believe, this even gets better...

From the two ladies that I just talked about, I'm now at the first class on the 2nd; the hostess is Faith. I've set up my display and am meeting and greeting the guests. Now, Shelley (the other booking on the 28th) comes in. She practically runs up to me, catalog in hand—the one she's bringing from the last party, and says: "Christie, Christie, I need your autograph!" Of course, I'm thrilled to see Shelley; I meet and greet her with a handshake or hug, and autograph her book. Now, the other guests who have already arrived are watching this. They've not met me before, and most likely don't know Shelley. But now they are in awe, wondering who this "famous" (why else would someone want an autograph?) demonstrator is!

Your catalogs are a business expense, but by using these tips, you'll discover they're not really expensive, but actually very valuable to your guests, and to you, as they add more bookings to your book!

Your catalogs are a business expense, but by using these tips, you'll discover they're not really expensive, but actually very valuable to your guests, and to you, as they add more bookings to your book!

Hostess Planning Packages

The three pieces of paper I've just discussed are for every guest at your demonstrations. The next *paper* to talk about is a *package* that you'll want everyone to take home with them. This is your package of planning materials for future classes. Perhaps your company provides a nice, large, brightly decorated envelope for all this literature. Regardless of what your company provides, be positive you provide this package to all new hostesses—on site at the present party.

As a hostess, I couldn't believe that when one of my friends told our demonstrator she wanted to schedule a class, the demonstrator replied: "Great, I'll call you to get a time, and then I'll mail you some information." I don't know if the show was ever held—or even scheduled! I know *I* didn't get an invitation. When a guest is ready to schedule, like my friend was, be prepared with your calendar and *Hostess Planning Package.* Even if you're not in a position to do a thorough hostess planning session (setting an appointment to go over the information later is usually best anyway), she needs to have a package in her hands *before* she leaves. Or, chances are, she'll change her mind before you call her back. On a practical financial note, mailing these packages can be expensive! Yet another reason to bring 'em along!

Being prepared at the show with this package is a powerful way to convey: "I'm serious about working with you to have a great presentation." If you're not prepared when the new hostess schedules—or wants to schedule—she'll likely have the same lackadaisical attitude about planning her event. This package of papers should be the first paper work you pack *and display.*

You read that last sentence correctly; I suggest you display the *Hostess Planning Package* as if it were one of your products, because it is! Remember earlier in this Segment when I talked about using the *Order Form*— specifically to book and recruit with the circles? When someone "orders" you to come to their home, this is the item they take home with them. Additionally, when you have an attractive package and it's on or near your display table, as guests look at your products, they'll look at the *Hostess Planning Package.* My suggestion is to bring packages for at least five new bookings and display two or three of them.

Note, the word "Package." The items for planning a class need to be all put together in a package format, like an envelope. Perhaps your company provides this as a sales tool. If not, purchase large envelopes at an office supply or keep reading for other ideas. If you choose the envelope, you can print on them yourself. Either way, I still embellish the envelopes with some of Jenny B's (thebooster.com) stickers.

I've seen some very creative *Hostess Planning Packages.* One suggestion is to use a regular office manila file folder either inside the envelope or as a stand alone so the hostess can keep everything in her own filing cabinet. A consultant who did a demonstration at my home provided all my supplies in a very colorful school report cover—the kind with no prongs in the middle and pockets on each side. If you are using a specific color to promote your personal icon, and can get report covers in that color, you're image is reinforced in your hostess' mind (refer to *The Name Game: Personal Icon).*

Now that the literature is in an envelope or other package, how do you position the paper to entice more bookings? If I were to offer you a business-looking envelope versus a fun, wrapped envelope, which would you choose? Most go for the wrapping. Consider wrapping your envelopes so when you present the *Hostess Planning Package* to the new hostess she feels like she's getting a present—she is! Or, you can make it easier by tying some ribbons and bows around the envelope. You can also purchase decorated, see-through plastic bags as a wrapping.

If you or your company offers *booking gifts*, I put the gift inside the decorated bag. This way, guests know the gift is connected with a booking. If booking gifts are not something you use and you want to add more enticement, you can add your own valuable and inexpensive gift. A gift can range from recipe cards to candy bars to small samples of products. The way you position this package and gift will help you add even more bookings.

I've discovered we all love handouts—handouts are a good example of a very valuable, inexpensive gift. Providing these for everyone at your classes takes away from their value; instead, include one in the *Presentation Planning Package*.

I've discovered we all love handouts—handouts are a good example of a very valuable, inexpensive gift. Providing these for everyone at your classes takes away from their value; instead, include one in the Presentation Planning Package.

While teaching a fun technique, recipe, or idea all you need to say is,

> "I've created written instructions for _____ ; they are included in this [hold up your Presentation Planning Package] hostess present. When you schedule a class with me, you get to take this present home with you!"
>
> I also suggest giving a copy to today's hostess. She's surprised and she feels special!

The other valuable gift I place in each hostess package is recruiting literature. Every hostess should have the opportunity to review information about joining your team. However, if you're just throwing brochures in every package and not talking with your hostess, you might as well just throw the brochures in a wastebasket.

Instead, when you review the materials at a hostess planning session--in person or on the phone--draw her attention to this. If she says, "I'm not interested," assure her this way:

> "Most hostesses usually aren't *initially* interested in joining our team. After all, I'm sure you love what you're doing

right now (being a stay-at-home mom, school teacher, bus driver, bank manager, etc.). However, after my hostesses read the brochure they realize they know someone who might want to know more information. Sometimes this is one of the guests you'll invite.

So, would you mind doing us all a favor? Take just two minutes to review the brochure and then please pass it on to your friend. Otherwise, I'll be happy to collect it from you when I get to your home."

Let's dissect this dialog. First, I always assume people love what they are doing! Never put them down. I've actually heard consultants say to guests: "You work as a waitress; you really should join my company; you'll make a lot more money!" The biggest problem with this tactic is you're attacking a customer. You're making her feel like what she does is not important.

Secondly, how do you know how much money she makes? She might even make more money than you depending on the kind of restaurant she works in. The difference with her income is that it's linear (and honestly a lot less in most cases); she gets paid once and is not building equity in her own business. Further, she doesn't have the chance of sharing a business opportunity and thus a substantial down line with reproductive, residual profits. If she likes what she's doing, she'll tell you. And if she isn't happy, she'll let you know that also. The key is to let her tell you, not vice versa.

Next, did you see how I *leap frogged* over her and asked her to read it with someone else in mind? Sometimes when we "take things away" from a person, she'll want it even more! Remember the story of Adam and Eve; they had everything but the fruit from one tree. And, wouldn't you know, that's just the fruit Eve just had to have! So, if you "take away" the opportunity from the hostess and ask her to read it with a friend in mind, she'll often do this. Remember, women tend to do for others what they do not do for themselves. And as they do something for someone else, like reading a brochure, they might realize they are indeed the *someone* in need!

Lastly, notice how I said I'd collect the information from her when I got to her home? What I'm conveying is *this is a valuable piece of literature*. I want it back even if you don't want it." The reason I want it back is not to save money on having to buy more brochures (that is an important aside), but it's to show her the *value of the brochure.*

The *Presentation Planning Package* is the best gift I know of for every guest to take "home in her hand" (refer to Segment on *The Power of Props – Taking Props Home.*

Recruiting Papers
You just read how to position your recruiting literature in *Hostess Presentation Packages.* Let's give some ideas for using this powerful paper at your demonstrations when you distribute it to selected guests; hostesses are not the only people you'll talk to about your opportunity. While I always tell my business story using products as props, I want to have something tangible to hand to guests who express interest or who I want to talk with individually. Many consultants miss recruiting possibilities because they give general opportunity information and fail to follow through on an individual basis. The potential of recruiting paper can be your *crutch* to selecting certain people.

Always have sufficient recruiting literature with you—at and away from shows—but treat this paper as if it were worth millions; it is! When I present the information, the people who I've chosen or who have requested know they are special people. In other words, everyone at a show is not given the business plan on paper. They must ask for more information (most don't do this) or I personally choose them.

Refer back to *The Power of Props: Seasonal Props* where I gave the example of using plastic "fill and thrill" Easter Eggs. You can use the same dialog to introduce your opportunity. Rather than hand everyone an egg that leads into their participating in the demonstration, do the *TWIST* and give only a select two or three guests an egg after the demonstration. You can do this discreetly in a one-on-one conversation, or you can publicly present the eggs by saying:

> "I have a couple of eggs that I want to go home with some of you. Let's see, Ginger would you take care of an egg for me? And Lauralee, I have one for you, would you like it?" Now, on the inside of these eggs, you have a foil wrapped (gold is best for the "golden egg") chocolate egg along with a note that says, 'If you're wanting to 'hatch' a new business to add $$ to your nest egg, call me.' "
>
> Include your name and phone number.

This is a fun *TWIST* where the people feel important; they know

95

that not everyone received this present. But you still need to follow through. The egg or paper will not recruit; only you can do that.

Here's another idea I used many, many times. It's an easy idea for the *gutless recruiters*; those who, like I was in the beginning, didn't know what to say or how to say it. I put my recruiting literature in a fun envelope decorated with stickers. This doesn't have to be a large envelope, just something that fits nicely. I added a note:

> Of all the guests I met today, you're the one I'd dream of having on my team. Read this brochure before you go to bed tonight. Put it under your pillow and sleep on it. I'll call you within 24 hours. Sweet Dreams!

This is a fun way to introduce the information; remember: only you can do the follow through—be sure you do or you'll lose the impact.

The many kinds of paper you'll use to book more classes and recruit more people can be endless and varied. Remember, paper only has potential. The real power lies in you, your personality, service, and follow through as you "do" the activities to book and recruit.

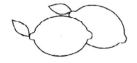

Segment Twelve

The Party's Over

The party might be over, but the fun has just begun. You have done a fabulous presentation and provided true service, not simply taken orders. And you've also met new friends, customers, hostesses and consultants! This is the beauty and the benefit of direct sales; our business is built on *and grows with* relationships! In sales, we hear the term, "closing the sale." In home demonstrations, the "sale is never closed" because the relationship is always ongoing. Guests know that you are now their service representative and have your contact information. They've learned valuable information in a fun way. Many have "hired" you to come to their home or office to service their families and friends.

In direct sales, our business is built on— and grows with— relationships! Whenever anyone mentions your company name or your product category, these people will remember—and hopefully revere—you.

So, after the people are not in physically in front of you, how do you stay "in front of them" mentally and emotionally? Another sales slogan is "service after the sale." This, coupled with your personal icon, will establish you in their minds and hearts. Whenever anyone mentions your company name or your product category, these people will remember—and hopefully revere—you.

Delivering Customer Service—Not Just Products

In the "old days" of the home party plan concept, guests would place orders, I'd order them through my company on a hard-copy invoice, and a week or so later the products would be delivered to me. I had the responsibility to sort products by party and then deliver the orders to the hostess. In today's party plan world, most orders are done over the Internet and shipped directly to the hostess and/or customer. Essentially, once you leave a class, you never have to have any contact with your guests and/or hostesses. To me, that's a sad scenario, and would not only close the sale but also many doors of opportunity! While this system has certainly streamlined our responsibilities as consultants, it has taken away an opportunity to see a hostess' face light up when we present her with a huge bag of products that she earned.

Further, in the old days, I also was able to personally make sure that all party orders were fulfilled correctly. This provided an added personal touch that helped to build my business. Today, while the new systems are certainly efficient, they're impersonal. And while I don't want to revert to the past, as far as service goes, it's not always *effective* at building your business with that personal touch; unless you do the *TWIST*...

With the *TWIST*, you'll see that you can actually have better follow through and more effective contact with your hostesses and guests. And you'll have the time you would have normally spent to pack and deliver to book and recruit more. Thus, you'll be more efficient as well as effective.

In the first segment of this book, *Pre-Presentation*, right on the first page of this book, I taught the concept of writing a *Thank You Note* as soon as the party is scheduled. This, you'll remember, thanks the hostess in advance for having a great show. As this book ends, my suggestion is another *Thank You* note to the hostess for having her class with you. In this note, I reiterate the gifts she's earned. Make a big long list of these! Let her literally see the items that she didn't pay anything for. Or, let her know she only paid $_____ for $_____ amount of merchandise. When you highlight this, she sees the value in her hosting the presentation and looks forward to the next one.

Also write down the expected delivery date of her shipment. The turn around time for an order is different for each company. If she had a class with one company whose turn around time was three days, and your company's is three weeks, she's going to be calling you at the end of ten days upset because she doesn't have the product. Give a realistic expectation—people don't mind the wait if they're notified in advance. In this note, I also include another magnet from TheBooster.com.

After you know (if you can track the order on line) or think the order has arrived, call the hostess to be sure everything arrived and the order was perfect. Your hostess is not a consultant. Even if she did end up joining your team, for this event, you were the consultant. If she has a problem with the order, she might call you when she gets around to it. She'd be pretty happy if you called her first! If there is a problem, instruct her how to call your customer service department or whatever steps are necessary to remedy the situation.

Ten days to two weeks after you know the hostess has the products, call every customer (both those who were in attendance and those who were not) to be sure they love what they've received. I can already hear the "but I don't have time to make these calls." If you've been in the industry for more than ten years, you probably know the hours spent packing, delivering, and inventorying orders. If you're new, imagine your house filled with boxes and products and spending hours and hours on this task. Now, be so grateful that instead all you have to do is pick up the phone, thank her for the order, and see that she loves what she purchased.

This call is for *customer service*. Part of customer service is to allow your customer the opportunity of being a hostess and/or a consultant. Time and again, as I do personal coaching with consultants, I hear they make "customer service calls" to check on the product but feel like they're intruding to invite her to be a hostess or consultant. Do you think Ed McMahon ever tells the American Family Publishers® people: "I don't think it's a good idea to go surprise the winner with her millions of dollars; she might be busy. I might interrupt her. She might get mad if I ring her doorbell." Of course, this would be ludicrous! People love gifts; they love money; they love you as a consultant. Don't talk yourself out of success and penalize your customers; that is so selfish! Here are some words you might use after you introduce yourself and verify that the order has been received and she's pleased:

> "Emelia, I'm so glad you love your new _____.
> You seem so excited about the product, you sound like you want to tell the world! My offer for you to be a hostess is still open .....
>
> Here's another for the people who you've not met:
>
> "Nancy, you sound really pleased with _____.
> Because we weren't able to personally meet, I am willing to come to your home to demonstrate _____ (your product/company name) so you and your friends can see a live presentation."

Will all these people jump up and down and say "yes, yes!"? Of course not. These calls do give you a chance to connect with customers and also build your business bank (this is discussed in the *Lemon Aid Deed Alphabet* pages 18-20).

Be prepared to soothe and help customers when you talk to them— they might not have their order yet. In most cases, the hostess just hasn't gotten around to making the delivery. When a guest hasn't received an order, who does she think is holding it up? She thinks it's you or your company. It doesn't dawn on her that her hostess might have it. When you make these calls, if she hasn't received

Part of customer service is to allow your customer the opportunity of being a hostess and/or a consultant.

the order, you can suggest that she go to the hostess' home to pick it up or just call the hostess. This call can save your reputation. As a guest, my hostess friends held up a lot of my orders…

On the other hand, your company might not yet have transitioned to *direct hostess delivery*. If this is the case, or if you fill the orders on site, you can still do these calls. Give your customers a couple of weeks to have used the products, once they've received them, and then phone.

You can do dozens and dozens of other activities to keep connected with your hostesses and customers. Again, I refer you to the *Lemon Aid Deed Alphabet*.

Business Brag Book

Lastly, if you can get together with your hostess and take a picture of her holding or using her hostess gifts, you can add this photo along with testimonials and thank you notes from your hostesses and guests to your *Business Brag Book*. I get double photos developed and send her a copy as well. You can take this *Brag Book* to all your classes so that potential hostesses and recruits can see you are the picture of success and so they can picture themselves as a hostess or a team member with you!

Segment Thirteen

Presentations For ...

You've read dozens of ideas for adding more bookings to your book. Ultimately, these bookings will become profits in your bank account. As a final *TWIST*, let's take our eyes off of profits and examine what our home presentations are really about. My good friend, Pattie Chwalek taught me: "When you take your eyes off the dollars, they'll fall in your wallet."

Products

Our presentations are very much about our products. If we had no company to represent with quality products, there would be no need for a presentation. At our home parties, a guest does not have to wonder what color or shape an item is: she can see, touch, smell, and sometimes taste our wares. Further, she is able to participate in the presentation so when she has the products in her home, she'll have more ideas of how to use them.

The home party method is the most basic as well as futuristic marketing plan in existence.

Several current home party companies actually began by selling via retail methods. After realizing that people didn't see a product's value or know how to use it, they converted to a home party marketing method so consumers would have the opportunity of free or very low-cost education in a fun, relaxed environment.

The products a consumer can learn about and purchase are varied. From learning how to preserve family photos to creating personalized greeting cards to decorating a comfortable home, to preparing simple meals to repairing a kitchen faucet...the list goes on and on...

Plan

The home party method is the most basic as well as futuristic marketing plan in existence. Years ago this idea was introduced to demonstrate products (many of which were initially unknown and new to the market, which is why many new products today use this method) with a unique *TWIST:* group marketing with one-on-one service built by word-of-mouth advertising, with hostess rewards, and consultant profits. Essentially, every person touched in the Home Party Plan marketing chain would gain more as she shared.

The concept back then was also built around a social theme. At that time, women—who were and continue to be the target audience—

enjoyed visiting and shopping in a relaxed, fun atmosphere. Now, in the 21st Century, our lifestyles are dramatically different since the conception of the home parties in the 1950s. Our calendars are over booked, yet our hearts are still in our homes. We desire the convenience of catalog or on-line shopping yet we demand personalized service. Further, we have a desire to keep in touch with neighbors, family, and friends as well as a thirst for continuing education. And, all this must be accomplished with a limited schedule and/or budget. Attending home parties where a consultant is cognizant of customers' individual needs is really the all-inclusive answer.

Some companies who have experienced successes with the home-party concept in the past and feel that their businesses are not growing have reverted to selling their products in a retail setting. While corporations have their reasons for this, it's a sad scenario. This dual-marketing effort conveys to the public and to consultants in and out of their companies that the home party industry is not thriving. Consultants feel this. I believe that a business stops growing when consultants think—and thus believe—"I can't book classes anymore." This negative thinking flows over to their presentations, guests feel their "panicked pressure" and say "no to bookings," recruiting is stunted and sales are flat. Thus, companies undergo sales declines (they need to be profitable to stay in business) and they do the *TWIST* in what I believe is the wrong direction. This cycle can end with the *Booking Breakthrough...*

Promotions

Yes, parties are about *products* distributed through a proven marketing and distribution *plan* where the consultant *profits*. Much of this is done through *promotions*. This is normally in the form of a hostess gift program. Rather than spending millions of dollars on advertising, companies use that budget to provide incentives for hostesses to invite family and friends to their home so we can educate and service them, and eventually sell products and recruit new consultants. Other promotions are in the form of specially priced or limited released items for hostesses, guests, and customers.

When a consultant hears of these promotions, she is so excited to tell her friends and customers. Her enthusiasm wanes when she does not get a similar response as she makes these calls. In my consulting sessions, demonstrators cannot believe why someone wouldn't want to take advantage of these promotions. So I give an illustration:

You and I love Chinese food, so we go to the all-you-can-eat buffet at a local restaurant. We spend two hours there feasting; we are literally stuffed! We decide to go to the mall to walk off some of the calories. As we're walking, we go past a new restaurant. The sign says, "All you can eat—FREE!!" Would we go in and partake of this promotion? Probably not; even though FREE is about as good as it gets! You see, we're not hungry! Sometimes we can offer the best promotions and incentives but we're trying to feed people who are stuffed!! As consultants, we should be willing to acknowledge their lack of hunger and ask their permission to keep in touch when they'll be hungry again.

Let's do a *TWIST* on this scenario. We go to lunch, all I have is a salad, which is rather tasty and I'm satisfied for a while. Now we go to the mall, we smell cinnamon rolls baking. We are salivating. Our noses carry our toes to the food court...only to find a lock on the door. The employees are having a party and are not open for business, even though they are available and we're hungry!

If you do have promotions and know of people who are hungry for them, but you have a lock on your business, you also have frustrated customers!

If you do have promotions and know of people who are hungry for them, but you have a lock on your business, you also have frustrated customers!

This is one step to have a booking breakthrough, let's knock down the barrier as we learn what presentations are really about...

Booking Breakthrough

To break down this barrier, consider this scenario: As you open your e-mail box today, you 're excited to see a message from the president of your company. After clicking on the message you're surprised to read:

> "Thank you for being a wonderful consultant with our company. You have a great future! By the way, as of next month, our company will no longer be sponsoring a gift program for hostesses."

What are you feeling right now? Are you already thinking of switching to another company with a hostess plan that's bigger and better? Are you mad? Are you ready to quit? If you're still committed to your company and its mission, and yet the hostess gift program is being eliminated, will you still be able to stay in business?

Well, I doubt you'll ever get a message like this. When I pose the last question to live Lemon Aid Learning audiences, people respond unanimoušly with: "No, we won't be in business without a hostess gift program."

Next, I ask them to think of retail establishments that sell a product category like they do. Not the same products because most Home Party companies have unique, higher-quality merchandise. So, if a consultant sells candles, I ask if there are retail companies that sell candles. In just about every case the answer is: "Yes, people can purchase my category or product at a retail store." Next I ask if the retail stores have a hostess program. As much as I travel, I've yet to see this type of an incentive. And then my response: "Retail stores are in business without hostess promotions; why would you be out of business if you didn't offer these gifts?"

You see, the secret of the booking breakthrough is to pretend you have no crutch to lean on, no incentives. What you have to offer— and no one does this like you do—is a proven product with superior service. Once I realized that my superb service could stand alone without hostess incentives, and that I could offer people "me" as a proven product (remember how people can order "you"), I broke through my booking barrier. I became confident—not cocky. I knew when I got the "nos" that people were not saying they didn't want me as a person. They simply were not hungry for what I had to feed them, or they didn't like what was on the menu! I knew they'd be hungry someday and I kept in touch with them appropriately. And I learned some "no's" meant they didn't want me to keep in touch with them. I respected that as well. The key is I kept moving on. I didn't allow the barrier to go up again.

Have you come to realize that Presentations are not only about Profit$, even though that's the title of the book? Presentations are not even just about our products. While we all offer unique products in terms of quality and concept, people could probably buy "wanna bees" at a retail outlet, on the Internet or through a catalog. And, believe it or not, Presentations are not always about promotions—remember FREE doesn't mean anything to people who aren't hungry.

Okay, now you know all the things that Presentations are not about. So, what are they about? Home Party Presentations with their wonderful products, fun and educational demonstrations, and valuable incentives—when it comes right down to it—really are all about...

People

As you go back and reread the last hundred plus pages of this book, you'll see that everything was based on and focused around *people*. From learning about guests and their lifestyles and meeting them over the phone before you meet them in person; to recognizing them for bringing a requested item to a *Featured Attraction*; to honoring them with the information you have on their *Getting to Know More About You* slip everything in this book is really about *People*. And when you *focus on the people* at your polished presentations, they'll be excited about the promotions and products. And you, in return for paying attention to *people* and their wants, needs, and interests, you will indeed make **Profits!** And in the Home Party industry, as we build equity in our own businesses, we really become more than profitable; we become **Prosperous!**

Appendix

Please note that all the material herein is copyrighted by Lemon Aid Learning Adventures™. However, as the owner of this book, you have permission to photocopy the following attachments—*Guest List* and *Guest Log*—for your own personal use and for your hostesses.

Please do not copy for any other use or for any other persons.

FREE LEMON AID!

Quench your thirst for more customers, hostesses, recruits, and strong team members on a continual basis. Join our FREE Internet list! Visit our website at www.lemonaidlady.com for details

Hostess Name _____ Demo Date _____ Time _____

Address _____ City _____ State _____ Zip _____

Phone _____ E-mail _____

Name _____	Name _____	Name _____
Address _____	Address _____	Address _____
City _____	City _____	City _____
State _____ Zip _____	State _____ Zip _____	State _____ Zip _____
Phone _____	Phone _____	Phone _____
Name _____	Name _____	Name _____
Address _____	Address _____	Address _____
City _____	City _____	City _____
State _____ Zip _____	State _____ Zip _____	State _____ Zip _____
Phone _____	Phone _____	Phone _____
Name _____	Name _____	Name _____
Address _____	Address _____	Address _____
City _____	City _____	City _____
State _____ Zip _____	State _____ Zip _____	State _____ Zip _____
Phone _____	Phone _____	Phone _____
Name _____	Name _____	Name _____
Address _____	Address _____	Address _____
City _____	City _____	City _____
State _____ Zip _____	State _____ Zip _____	State _____ Zip _____
Phone _____	Phone _____	Phone _____
Name _____	Name _____	Name _____
Address _____	Address _____	Address _____
City _____	City _____	City _____
State _____ Zip _____	State _____ Zip _____	State _____ Zip _____
Phone _____	Phone _____	Phone _____
Name _____	Name _____	Name _____
Address _____	Address _____	Address _____
City _____	City _____	City _____
State _____ Zip _____	State _____ Zip _____	State _____ Zip _____
Phone _____	Phone _____	Phone _____
Name _____	Name _____	Name _____
Address _____	Address _____	Address _____
City _____	City _____	City _____
State _____ Zip _____	State _____ Zip _____	State _____ Zip _____
Phone _____	Phone _____	Phone _____

Hostess ——————— **Phone** ——————— **Demo Date** ———————

Customer	Phone	Address/City/Zip Code	Product Total	Total due	Paid
1.					
2.					
3.					
4.					
5.					
6.					
7.					
8.					
9.					
10.					
11.					
12.					
Totals Page ___ of ___					

Congratulations on a fun demonstration! You only need sales of _____ and _____ demos scheduled to qualify for your goal of _____.   Please have all orders/payments by _____.

Copyright 1998 CANet Consulting P.O. Box 1720 Lake Dallas, TX 75065   1-888-358-3001

Are you Thirsting for more Hostesses, Customers, and Recruits?

Invite The Lemon Aid Lady to quench that thirst with classes tailored to you...

Lemon Aid Learning Adventures™ now offers a variety of classes...in different formats...to help you book more demonstrations, sell to more customers, and greatly expand your team with new recruits and more leaders.

On-site Classes
We've adapted our popular Lemon Aid Learning Adventures for team meetings. For groups of 50 or more, we'll come to your location with a two-hour presentation custom-tailored to your company, area, and team needs. Call for details.

Team Telephone Talk
If your group is small, take heart! We offer a 45-minute team talk by phone.

Lemon Aid One-on-One
Personal coaching, Lemon Aid style! In personal, half-hour phone sessions, Christie will help you *twist* your personal Sour Situations into Sweet Successes and Juicy Profits.

Three Options. A myriad of topics..
We offer a wide variety of presentations, including:

Sales
- Where to Find Customers when you Run out of Family and Friends
- Presentations for Profit$
- Family Fortunes without Family Feuds
- There's No Place Like Working From Home

Leadership
- From Parenting Your Team to Mentoring Your Team
- Lemon Aid for Leaders
- Totally Terrific Teams
- Opportunity Meetings with a *TWIST*
- When Life Give You Lemons, Start a Lemon Aid Stand

Lemon Aid Learning Adventures. Creating Sweet Successes and Juicy Profits!

Lemon Aid Learning Adventures
P.O. Box 1720
Lake Dallas TX 75065
940-498-0995 www.lemonaidlady.com

Add more Sweet Successes and Juicy Profits with these other Lemon Aid™ Books and Tapes!

The Lemon Aid Lead Alphabet: Where to Find Customers when you run out of Family and Friends

Quench your thirst for new business with the ABCs of generating sales leads. This 115-page book is written in an easy-to-use, reference-style format. No need to read the book from cover to cover. Simply turn to any page for easy, creative, no-cost ideas for finding people who want and need your product or service.
$19.95

The Lemon Aid Deed Alphabet

Once you have located leads, what deeds do you need to do to convert them to committed customers? Written in the same format as the *Lead Alphabet*, this 120-page book will teach you what to do to keep your customers committed to YOU and how to it.
$19.95

Totally Terrific Team Themes

Are your team meetings a treat to plan? Do team members look forward to attending the meetings? Does performance increase after a meeting is held? The answers to all these questions will be a firm "yes" when you plan your meetings using the themes in this book.
$19.95

The Lemon Aid Lead Alphabet Tape Series

Do you own the *Lemon Aid Lead Alphabet: Where to Find Customers when you run out of Family and Friends?* Have you attended a live Lemon Aid Learning Adventure with the Lemon Aid Lady? Now you can combine the best of both experiences and hear NEW ideas never before taught in a live session or published in the book. This nearly four-hour audio tape set will teach you the A-to-Zs of finding customers in unlikely places with innovative *TWISTS*.
$55.95

Prices and product availability subject to change without notice.

Lemon Aid Learning Adventures. Creating Sweet Successes and Juicy Profits!

Lemon Aid Learning Adventures
P.O. Box 1720
Lake Dallas TX 75065
940-498-0995 www.lemonaidlady.com